SPECIES WITH AMNESIA: OUR FORGOTTEN HISTORY

Robert Sepehr

Printed in the United States of America

First Printing, 2015

ISBN: 978-1-943494-04-0

Atlantean Gardens
5334 Lindley Ave #133
Encino, CA 91316

www.AtlanteanGardens.org

able of Contents

Introduction

Highly advanced civilizations have been here before us, just to be destroyed by some great global catastrophe. But for each race that has died out, another has taken its place, with a selected few holding on to the memories and sacred knowledge of the past race. In our vanity we think we have discovered some of the great truths of science and technology, but we are in fact only just beginning to rediscover the profound wisdom of past civilizations. In many ways, we are like an awakening *Species with Amnesia*, yearning to reclaim our forgotten past.

Chapter 1

Experts in the mainstream media constantly reassure us that science has, for all intents and purposes, solved the basic mysteries regarding the origins of humanity. Academics insist that we are the relatively recent culmination of a gradual process of random mutations via a single mechanism called natural selection, first proposed by Charles Darwin around 150 years ago.(23) This theory describes a generally linear progression from tree-dwelling monkey to bipedal human, passing from pro-simian (pre-monkey), to monkey, to great ape, and finally to humans. (10) As modern science makes more and more advances in the illuminating fields of human genetics and archeology, however, we find that our most celebrated explanation of how man came to be is no longer adequate. Museums, documentary film producers, and schools hire paleo-artists, armed with paintbrushes, to produce imaginary versions of humanity's direct evolutionary ancestors: our supposed ape-like relatives.

The fact that these works of art do not correspond to any fossils should constitute a serious problem for the formally educated anthropologists who insist on the "man-from-monkey" model of human origin. The lack of any correspondence does not show that the theory is necessarily false, but it is fair to point out that what turns up in the media, all too often does not turn up in the archeological records.

One interesting and creative method some "scholars" have employed to overcome this problem is to "produce" the fossils they cannot find. Piltdown Man, possibly the biggest scandal in the history of science, is probably the most infamous example of the falsification and fabrication of our prehistory.(25)

Charles Dawson was an amateur archaeologist who lived in southern England, near Sussex. In 1889, Dawson co-founded the Hastings and St Leonards Museum Association, one of the first museum friends groups established in Britain. He volunteered, as a member of the Museum Committee, to take charge of the acquisition of artifacts and documents. After several finds, he was soon elected a fellow of the Geological Society and, a few years later, to the Society of Antiquaries of London in 1895.

In 1908, workmen are said to have presented him with curious bone fragments which they claimed to have found while working in a gravel pit near the town of Piltdown. The discovery piqued Dawson's interest, and he soon began his own excavation in the pit. Dawson found further fragments of the skull and took them to Arthur Smith Woodward, keeper of the geological department at the British Museum. Greatly interested by the finds, Woodward accompanied Dawson to the site, where between June and September 1912 they recovered more fragments of the skull and half of the lower jaw bone. Given the proximity of the skull fragments and the jawbone to each other, Dawson concluded they must have belonged together as part of the very same skull. (14)

This was an unusual find, because when combined, the skull displayed characteristics of both man and ape. The jaw was ape-like, whereas the upper skull fragments were definitely human. If the jaw and skull fragments did come from the same creature, then they had found the "missing link". (14,25) That is the term given to the transitional species Darwinists expected to fill the evolutionary gap in the fossil record between man and his simian ancestors.(10)

In December, 1912 Woodward displayed a reconstruction of the skull at a meeting of the Geological Society of London. He argued that it was the skull of a man, whom he called Piltdown man, after the location where it had been found. He further argued that it came from a human who had lived about half a million years ago, during the Lower Pleistocene period. It was promptly billed by the mainstream media as the "missing link" between humans and great apes.(25)

FIGURE 1

Woodward's fantastic claim caused an enormous stir both within the scientific community and with the general public. From the start, paleontologists and anatomists from the Smithsonian Institution, and from Europe, felt the jawbone and skull were too dissimilar to belong together. The jaw, many skeptics pointed out, looked far more apish than one would expect to find attached to a high-vaulted, human skull. Woodward's backers in academia, as well as the media, however, eventually won out and the new species entered the academic textbooks as Eoanthropus dawson, or "Dawson's Dawn Man."(12) Over the next few years, more fossil objects turned up in the Piltdown pit: animal bones, an object that looked like a cricket bat, and two more skulls. In 1916, Dawson died, leaving Woodward as the main advocate for the Piltdown man.

For close to four decades, the scientific community accepted the Piltdown skull as an authentic artifact, and hailed it as the transitional link between ape and man.(25) As archeologists discovered more skeletons of 'early man', however, it became clear that the Piltdown Man radically differed from anything else in the fossil record. No other specimen shared its unusual traits. Therefore, finally, in 1953 a team of researchers at the British Museum (Kenneth Oakley, Wilfred Le Gros Clark, and Joseph Weiner) subjected the skull and jawbone to a rigorous series of tests. What they found sent shock waves across the scientific world: the Piltdown man was a fake!

"Piltdown Man Hoax Is Exposed," announced the New York Times on November 21, 1953.(1) "Part of the skull of the Piltdown man, one of the most famous fossil skulls in the world, has been declared a hoax by authorities at the British Natural History Museum," the article said.

Piltdown Man Named Hoax, Jolts Science

London, Nov. 21 (INS)—Three British scientists branded the famous "Piltdown man" a deliberate fake today and set off a controversy that may engage the scientific world for years to come.

FIGURE 2

The London Star headlines shouted, "The Biggest Scientific Hoax of the Century!"(25)

Using a fluorine-based test to date the skull, the researchers determined that the upper skull was thousands of years old. They also found that the jaw had been artificially stained with potassium dichromate to make it appear older. A second test, using nitrogen analysis, confirmed the results of the first test.(26)

The British Museum researchers revealed that someone must have taken the jawbone and teeth of a modern ape, probably an orangutan, and stained them to give them an ancient appearance. These artifacts, the ape jaw and the skull fragments, must have been planted at the Piltdown site and are now universally recognized as a hoax.

In 1922, Harold Cook officially discovered Nebraska Man in the Pleistocene deposits of Nebraska. A tremendous amount of literature arose around this next find, hailing it as the elusive "missing link" which allegedly roamed the Americas one million years ago.(27) Clarence Darrow used the evidence for Nebraska Man in the famous 1925 Scopes Monkey Trial in Dayton, Tennessee. Formally known as The State of Tennessee v. John Thomas Scopes, the Scopes Trial was an American criminal case in which a substitute high school teacher, John Scopes, was accused of teaching evolution in schools, in violation of existing law concerning how the subject of human origins may be taught in a state-funded school. William Jennings Bryan, for the prosecution, argued against the Darwinian model. A battery of "great scientific experts" stunned him with the "facts" of Nebraska Man. Mr. Bryan had no retort except to say that he thought the evidence was too scanty and to plead for more time. Naturally, the "experts" scoffed and made a mockery of him. After all, who was he to question the world's greatest scientific authorities?(12,13,14,15, 27)

But, what exactly did these authorities present as the scientific proof for Nebraska Man? A single tooth. Many of the top published scientists in the world examined this tooth and appraised it as proof positive of a prehistoric link, some even publishing illustrations of what Nebraska man and his habitat must have looked like. (14, 15, 27)

Years after the Scopes trial, the entire skeleton of the animal from which Nebraska man's tooth came was found. As it turned out, the tooth belonged to an extinct species of boar.(15) The "academic authorities," who had ridiculed Mr. Bryan for his supposed ignorance, had created an entire species of humanity out of the tooth of a pig. What an embarrassment to the scientific community and a noteworthy commentary on how preconceived notions of supposed ape-men influenced Darwinian hardliners to such a great degree. (13, 27)

The error received little publicity. Yet this court case provided precedent for all future matters concerning guidelines for what is to be allowed in classrooms concerning theories on human origins.(15) There is a lesson here concerning the reliability of so-called expert testimony, which is so often produced simply to manipulate and intimidate the layman who lacks the proper mainstream indoctrination.

A similar discovery, also based upon an animal's tooth, was the Southwest Colorado Man. It is now known that this particular tooth belonged to a horse, but like Nebraska man, the error has been all but forgotten and conveniently swept under the rug.(16) I did however manage to find an old article mentioning the discovery; here is a 1927 comment from *Time* magazine:

The "Southwestern Colorado Man," lately deduced from a set of Eocene teeth, was a myth, the teeth having proved to be those of an antique horse.(17)

How resourceful and imaginative the strict adherents of a particular theory can be. Give them a tooth, not necessarily even remotely human, and they can create an entire race of prehistoric humanity. To drive the point home, I will briefly tell of one more example of these hominoidal 'one-tooth wonders'. The naturalist, Dr. J.C.F. Siegfriedt, promoted this specimen, dubbed the "Montana Man", to much public fanfare.(18) He enlisted several local dentists to support his claims. In 1927, just months after its finding, other experts denounced the tooth upon which Siegfriedt based his Montana Man as the tooth of an extinct quadruped:

The discovery, in a coal mine on the windswept mountain slopes near Billings, MO, of a fossil molar tooth of human appearance, mixed in with fossil clams and lizards known to belong in the Eocene period, 50 to 60 million years ago, caused a great deal of newspaper talk last autumn. But experts were inclined to view the molar as that of euprotogonia, doglike Eocene quadruped with manlike teeth in its bearlike-horselike head.(18)

The next major find hailed as the elusive link came out of Africa. Lucy is the popular nickname name given to the famous African fossil skeleton that American anthropologist Donald Johanson found in Ethiopia in 1974. The discovery was described as the first known member of Australopithecus afarensis, which means southern ape. Dr. Johanson's girlfriend suggested she be named "Lucy," after the Beatles song, "Lucy in the Sky with Diamonds" which played repeatedly during the night of the discovery. (20)

Over the last forty years, universities that accept Federal or State funding have unanimously proclaimed the 3.2 million year old specimen the ancestor of all humanity. Lucy has become famous through broad dissemination in academic magazines, television shows, books, newspapers, and museums. But is Lucy really a direct ancestor to mankind? (21)

Dr. Charles Oxnard, Professor of Anatomy and Human Biology at the University of Western Australia, said of the Australopithecine (the group to which Lucy belonged):

"The various australopithecines are, indeed, more different from both African apes and humans in most features than these latter are from each other. Part of the basis of this acceptance has been the fact that even opposing investigators have found these large differences as they, too, used techniques and research designs that were less biased by prior notions as to what the fossils might have been."(22)

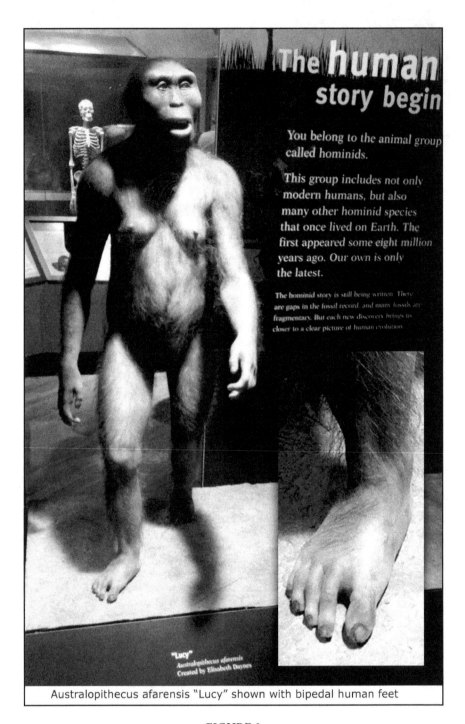

The **human** story begin

You belong to the animal group called hominids.

This group includes not only modern humans, but also many other hominid species that once lived on Earth. The first appeared some eight million years ago. Our own is only the latest.

The hominid story is still being written. There are gaps in the fossil record, and many fossils are fragmentary. But each new discovery brings us closer to a clear picture of human evolution.

"Lucy"
Australopithecus afarensis
Created by Elisabeth Daynes

Australopithecus afarensis "Lucy" shown with bipedal human feet

FIGURE 3

Upon my own inspection, in a formal classroom setting, it was immediately clear to me that this fossil was not the same as what was being sold to the public. The full-flesh recreations in museums around the world, of how Lucy supposedly looked, are complete fabrications, purely speculation, with little basis in reality. Artists with little or no experience or education in anthropology primarily construct these depictions. In the Michigan State University museum, they depicted her with human eyes, not ape eyes. The pictures all show a creature that walked upright (bipedal) and had the face, hands, and feet of a nearly-human species. Artistic renderings typically depict Lucy with human-like hands, and walking in an upright position on human-like feet. This is true for the models at the NY Museum of Natural History, the American Museum of Natural Sciences, the Museum of Man in San Diego, the National Museum of Anthology in Mexico City, the St. Louis Zoo, the University of NM, and Michigan State University. One can also readily find artistic depictions of Lucy in science textbooks, or on televised documentaries, that depict her walking in an upright position with human-like hands and feet.

However, these presentations are not scientific; they are tools of manipulation and falsified visual aids to demonstrate what the empirical evidence itself fails to show. Lucy's big toe looked like a thumb used to grasp with, not walk. While Lucy's founder strongly argues that Lucy walked bipedally, he has too much of a personal stake in the matter to be unbiased. He has become famous simply because he discovered Lucy.

The evidence against Lucy's bipedalism includes:

- As observed by Dr. Susman and Dr. Stern of the State University of NY at Stony Brook, Lucy's feet retained grasping tendencies with long and curved digits. (9)
- In 1993, anthropologist Christine Tardieu reported that Lucy had an undeveloped locking mechanism. Humans have a locking mechanism in our knees which allows us to stand comfortably upright for long periods. Lucy did not have that, so she certainly did not stand around nonchalantly, as she is depicted in the museums.
- In 1995, *Science News* reported that a partial skeleton of an A. af-

ricanus had been found "whose ape-like body was capable of only limited two-legged walking." It's pelvis was "generally ape-like in shape." (5)

- The *Journal of Human Evolution* reported that biochemical studies of the hip and thigh of the Australopithecus had concluded that it did not walk uprightly. (6)

- In 2000, *Nature* magazine reported, "Regardless of the status of Lucy's knee joint, new evidence has come forth that Lucy has the morphology of a knuckle-walker."(4)

- That same year *Science* magazine published and reported the same basic finding; Lucy "has the morphology that was classic for knuckle walkers."(3)

- In 2007, anthropologists at the Tel Aviv University, declared they had disproven the theory that Lucy (Australopithecus) is a common ancestor of humans:

The specific structure found in Lucy also appears in a species called Australopithecus robustus. The presence of the morphology in both the latter and Australopithecus afarensis and its absence in modern humans cast doubt on the role of [Lucy] as a common ancestor.(2)

Despite their ability to walk upright for short distances, primates represented by the "Lucy" fossil spent much of their time in trees, remaining very active climbers. In 2012, scientists published research that comprehensively analyzed two complete shoulder blades from an exceptionally well-preserved skeleton, from Ethiopia, of a 3-year-old Australopithecus afarensis girl dating back 3.3 million years. The arms and shoulders potentially yield insights on how well they climbed. The researchers found these bones had several details in common with those of modern apes, suggesting they lived at least part of the time in trees. For instance, the socket for the shoulder joint was pointed upward in both Australopithecus afarensis and today's apes, a sign of an active climber. In humans, these sockets face out to the sides. Lucy's adult shoulder sockets also faced upward, suggesting that, like modern apes, her species was equipped for tree-climbing. (11)

The cranial capacities of Australopithecus afarensis are the same, or smaller, than the chimpanzees of our day. They are short (maximum 130 cm. / 51 in.) and their feet are built for grasping and holding onto branches. Many other characteristics concerning details in their skulls, the closeness of their eyes, their sharp molar teeth, their mandibular structure, their long arms, and their short legs all constitute evidence that these creatures were not even remotely human and not very much different from modern apes.

Gary Sawyer and Mike Smith at the American Museum of Natural History in New York recently began work on a new reconstruction of Lucy's skeleton, with help from Scott Williams at New York University, who noticed something odd and proclaimed that:

"One of the [vertebra] fragments, which no one, including me, had really paid close attention to, looked fairly small to fit with the rest of Lucy's vertebral column."(24)

They started a comparative analysis and soon concluded that the fragment was too small. Their results showed, surprisingly, that the fragment may not have belonged to Australopithecus at all.(24) According to Scott Williams:

"We think we've solved this mystery. It seems that a fossil gelada baboon thoracic vertebra washed or was otherwise transported in the mix of Lucy's remains."(24)

In other words, one of the pieces of the Lucy fossil turns out to have belonged to a baboon, and somehow just happened to get mixed in with the rest of the discovery. Keep in mind that there was no sign of a baboon skeleton at the site where Lucy was discovered in 1974, yet this small detail had gone unnoticed for the last 40 years. I do not want to give off the impression that Lucy is another hoax, like the Piltdown man was, as there are other specimen samples that establish her as a legitimate species. I did want to mention this incident, however, since it underscores that the dominant Darwinian model for human evolution remains incomplete and still very much just a theory.

Let us now turn to Ardipithecus ramidus, or "Ardi", as he was nicknamed in September 1994. The first fossil found of this specimen was dated to 4.4 million years ago, more than a million years before Lucy (Australopithecus afarensis). Ardi had a small brain, measuring between 300cc and 350cc. This is slightly smaller than a modern bonobo or female chimpanzee brain; roughly 20% the size of the average modern human brain.(28)

In 2009, an internationally recognized biological anthropologist who specializes in the study of human origins, Kent State University Professor Dr. C. Owen Lovejoy, revealed some starting conclusions regarding this latest find:

"People often think we evolved from ancestors that look like apes, but no, apes.. evolved from ancestors that look like us,"(9)

This is a bold statement coming from someone with such a prominent reputation in mainstream Archeology. His primary claim to fame was work involving Lucy. To clarify his statement, Lovejoy continued:

"It has been a popular idea to think humans are modified chimpanzees, but from studying Ardipithecus ramidus, or 'Ardi,' we learn that we cannot understand or model human evolution from chimps and gorillas."(9)

Professor Lovejoy's analysis showed that the bones in Ardi's hands and wrists were not adapted to knuckle-walking, a style of movement common to gorillas and chimpanzees and assumed to have been used by the ancestral species to apes and humans. In other words, Lovejoy believes that because Ardipithecus had not evolved the hands and wrists of a knuckle-walker, no human ancestor ever walked on its knuckles, and chimpanzees and gorillas each evolved that trait after they had separated from the human lineage. So according to Lovejoy, man didn't descend from apes. What is closer to the truth is that our knuckle-dragging cousins descended from us.(9)

If this interpretation holds up, it could have a major impact on the field of primatology because it would overturn long-held ideas about how living apes can be used as models of humanity's earliest ancestors.

Darwin put forward his claim that human beings and apes descended from a common ancestor in his book, *The Descent of Man*, published in 1871. From that time until now, the followers of Darwin's proposal have tried to support and passionately promote this paradigm. But despite all the research that has been carried out, no unfalsified evidence has backed up this man-from-ape idea.(10)

There can be no doubt that, for all living organisms, evolution and/or adaption is a real and true phenomenon, when defined and observed as "change over time". However, change comes about in many ways, certainly in more ways than just haphazard mutation and natural selection, especially with regards to humanity. Darwinian theory, and it's mechanism of natural selection, is simply incomplete and, at least in the case of mankind, totally fails in effectively explaining the genesis of humans on this planet.

The fossil record does not indicate in any scientific way the linear progressive model of mankind's rise from small ape-like creatures (pro-simians), to monkeys, then to great apes, and finally to us. In fact, what is becoming clear, especially as more research is published in the field of genomics, is that mankind may actually be a composite being; a hybrid species.

Chapter 2

In 1950, the United Nations Educational, Scientific, and Cultural Organization (UNESCO) issued a statement asserting that all humans belong to the same species and that race is not a biological reality, but a myth. This statement summarized the findings of an international panel of cultural anthropologists, geneticists, sociologists, and psychologists(50). Many scientific discoveries have been made since 1950, especially in the field of human genetics, indicating that humanity is, biologically speaking, a hybrid species, and not one single "race".(29)

The most widely accepted model for the geographic origin and initial dispersal of anatomically correct humans is called the, "out-of-Africa" theory in the media, and the "replacement hypothesis", by anthropologists in the field. The predominant position in the scientific community argues for a single origin of modern humans in East Africa, who migrated out from there, and replaced other hominin populations by either killing them, or out-competing them for resources. A growing number of researchers, however, propose that North Africa, near the Mediterranean Sea, was more likely the original home of the human voyagers who theoretically first left the African continent.

The major competing hypothesis, called the multiregional origin theory, envisions world-wide gene flow and exchange, especially about 35,000 years ago, by modern humans interbreeding with various types of anatomically correct Homo erectus, Neanderthal, and other hominin populations around the globe. Many multiregionalists traditionally considered several possible locations for the cradles of civilization. Probably the most popular geographic hot-spot was near the arctic, at one time when climate conditions were favorable, possibly before a pole shift or other global cataclysm. Other hypothesized locations with many proponents are in and under Asia (Shamballa) and those exotic places eluded to in ancient myth, such as Atlantis, Mu, or Lemuria, now submerged under the melted glaciers of the ice age beneath the vast Atlantic, Pacific, and Indian oceans.

Although not many multiregional archeologists searching the world's oceans for submerged land masses, there is a growing body of conclusive genetic evidence which scientifically demonstrates that different anatomically correct hominin species interbred with modern humans and produced the viable hybrid offspring of mixed interspecies ancestry, which led to our current populations. (29, 34, 51, 52, 53, 54, 55, 56, 57, 58, 59, 60, 61)

The field of anthropology is fraught with contradictions, especially in regards to the archaic admixture in the human record, which I have personally experienced during my years in the California State University system. But the growing mountain of irrefutable evidence shows that different archaic hominid species mixed genes interracially, crossing their own species' genetic boundaries, and that this admixture is still detectable and influences humans today.(61) Hybridization, or the biological process by which individuals from genetically distinct populations (e.g., species, subspecies) mate and produce at least some viable offspring, is of great relevance to understanding the origins of biodiversity, especially in relation to human racial origins. The DNA evidence indicates that ancient humans participated in cross-species sex and exchanged genomic material which can now be measured, since we have learned how to map modern and archaic genomes. One recent tabloid headline touted that:

Ancient humans 'rampantly interbred' with Neanderthals and a mystery species in Lord Of The Rings-style world of different creatures. (80)

Although a bizarre, if not humorously phrased headline, there is truth in it's implications. This ice age antediluvian world often portrayed in movies such as *Lord of the Rings,* featuring great battles and romances between dwarfs, elves, giants and hobbits, can be better appreciated in light of scientific findings which prove that our ancestors indulged in interracial (cross-species) mating with multiple sub-races of different hominins. These findings include archaic DNA discovered in modern Africans, neither human nor Neanderthal, and not found in the genome of non-Africans.(29,30) DNA evidence shows that interbreeding between archaic and modern humans did indeed involve different species of archaic hominins. (61)

In 1998, the Michael Hammer lab published a paper which proposed a recent migration, around 35,000 years ago, of modern humans INTO Africa, and accounting for the majority of African Y chromosomes. The paper explains that Haplogroups A and B, found exclusively in Africa, were the product of admixture between archaic African hominids and the incoming, or back-migrating, modern humans who mated with them.(81)

Archaeologically, the presence of sites such as Dabban, with clear Upper Paleolithic links, in North Africa around 35,000 YBP supports the theory of a migration into Africa. Dabban is an early blade-and-burin industry of Libya, dating to 40,000-14,000 years ago, and is thought to be the oldest dated blade-and-burin industry of Upper Palaeolithic type. It clearly relates, in respects to stone tool technology, to the Upper Palaeolithic complex of Europe and the Near East.

From the paleobiological perspective, the Hofmeyr skull in South Africa dated at around 36,200 YBP clusters with Upper Paleolithic Eurasians and Europeans, which, again, suggests that Africa was peopled from Eurasia or Europe, not the other way around. Found in 1952, the Hofmeyr Skull is one of only a few African specimens of early modern humans dated to over 30,000 years. It is rather distinct from those of recent Sub-Saharan Africans, and more closely resembles traits from people who lived in Europe in the Upper Paleolithic period, at the same time as the Hofmeyr skull.(82) The skull demonstrates that humans arriving in Africa 36,000 years ago resembled those in early Europe, such as the Cro magnon specimen of the Pyrenees, with no primitive features of prognathism (protruding jaw). A 2007 paper proposed that the Hofmeyr cranium looks like "Upper Paleolithic (UP) Eurasians," or ice age Europeans, rather than the "recent, geographically proximate people,"; or modern Africans. The paper claimed, at a time when broad genomic sequencing data was unavailable, that this resemblance supported the out of Africa hypothesis.(82) Since then, published genetic findings have demonstrated the opposite scenario, one where modern genetics from outside of Africa entered the continent. Studies show that contemporary Europeans shared genetic continuity with ancient Europeans, but lack the genetic markers found in modern Africans. In other words, Europeans did not descend from Africans, but modern Africans are an admixture of upper paleolithic Europeans and an archaic species, possibly Homo heidelbergensis, whose DNA is not found in non-Africans.(88)

Scientific evidence refuting the popular theory of modern humanity's African genesis is becoming common knowledge among those few who are familiar with the most recent scientific papers published on the human Genome and how it compares to the other hominin genomes which have also now been sequenced.(32,61) Regrettably, within the mainstream press and academic circles, there is a conspicuous and, dare I say, deliberate vacuum when it comes to reporting on these studies and their controversial implications.(34) The Australian historian, Greg Jefferys, believes this agenda to eradicate the notion of race, for political rather than scientific reasons, which goes back decades:

◇◇◇

"The whole Out of Africa myth has its roots in the mainstream academic campaign in the 1990's to remove the concept of Race. When I did my degree they all spent a lot of time on the Out of

Africa thing but it's been completely disproved by genetics. Main-stream still hold on to it." (73)

◇◇◇

The evidence clarifying and defining race in modern humans, in a biolog-ical sense, is helping to shed light on what many years of politically motivated propaganda has obscured. An example is a very interesting paper, which traces the paternal lineage or Y-chromosomes (traceable genes passed down from father to son), published in 2012 and called "Re-Examining the 'Out of Africa' Theory and the Origin of Europeoids (Caucasians) in the Light of DNA Ge-nealogy." It concludes that sub-Saharan Africans did not leave Africa to colo-nize the rest of the world.(32) This extensive examination of 7,556 haplogroups confirmed that there were no African genetic markers in the non-African par-ticipants. So lacking was the sampling of African genetic involvement in any of the non-African test subjects that the researchers stated:

◇◇◇

The finding that the Europeoid haplogroups did not descend from "African" haplogroups A or B is supported by the fact that bearers of the Europeoid, as well as all non-African groups do not carry SNI's M91, P97, M31, P82, M23, M114, P262. (32)

◇◇◇

The conclusion that European haplogroups did not descend from the African haplogroups, evidenced by an absence of dozens of African genetic markers, makes it impossible to sustain any direct evolutionary link from modern Europeans to modern Africans. The researchers insist that their extensive study offers evidence compelling a re-examination of the validity of the Out-of-Africa concept. In fact, the researchers stated that:

◇◇◇

Not one non-African participant out of more than 400 individuals in the Project tested positive to any of thirteen 'African' sub-clades of haplogroup A. (32)

◇◇◇

They concluded that there was insufficient proof to substantiate African precedence in the Homo sapien tree, and claim there must be a more plausible explanation. Unfortunately, results such as these incite unfounded accusations of racism that have become increasingly common as the growing mountain of scientific evidence, especially in the field of genetics, challenges the prevailing hypothesis. Geneticists have not only mapped the entire human genome, including people native to every continent, but they have also successfully sequenced nearly complete genomes from very ancient remains, a task that, until recently, very few in my field thought possible. It is now a scientifically irrefutable fact that the "human species" contains a substantial quantity of DNA from other hominid populations not classified as Homo sapien; such as Neanderthal, Denisovan, African archaic, Homo erectus, and now even "Hobbit" (Homo floresiensis).(61)

The relationship between modern humans and archaic hominins, particularly Neanderthals, has been the subject of much ongoing debate. Neanderthals occupied most of Europe and parts of Western Asia from roughly 30-300 thousand years ago.(57) For part of this time, they coexisted with the first completely modern humans, commonly referred to as Cro magnon. Both mitochondrial (mtDNA) and nuclear DNA have been successfully extracted from Neanderthal fossils and sequenced.(59) These sequences have provided information about the appearance and speech capability of Neanderthals, as well as their phylogenetic relationship with modern humans. Analysis that compared a sequence of the Neanderthal genome with genomes of several modern humans concluded that Neanderthals contributed to the gene pools of all non-African populations, as well as the Masai of East Africa who have a small but significant fraction of Neanderthal DNA. Neanderthals contributed more DNA to modern East Asians than to modern Europeans, with a difference on the order of 40%, indicating that populations of Cro magnon and Neanderthal interbred some 35,000-27,000 years ago.(57,59) Similar tests on another archaic species, the Denisovans, named after their location of discovery in Siberia, have uncovered similar inherited genetic contributions to certain modern populations; 7% to Samoans and south east Asians.(58,61)

The discovery of the Denisovans further complicates the connection between an archaic hominin species and a modern human population. Denisovans fossil remains were discovered in East Asia, but the Denisovans show greater similarity to modern Melanesians than to East Asians. Although initial studies suggested that Denisovan ancestry appeared only in modern human populations from island Southeast Asia and Oceania, more recent studies suggest that Denisovan ancestry may be more widespread.(83)

An article published in the journal Nature, titled, "The complete genome sequence of a Neanderthal from the Altai Mountains", had interesting findings about Neanderthals, Denisovans and Native Americans. Native Americans carry both Denisovan and Neanderthal DNA, and more than Europeans. The Denisovan and Neanderthal DNA that they carry differs from that carried by Europeans.(84) Native Americans today indeed inherited their propensity for type 2 diabetes from their ancient Neanderthal ancestors who lived in the Altai Mountains. It also appears that this genetic predisposition did not carry forward to Europe.(85)

The overwhelming genetic evidence should end the anthropological debate over whether modern humans are a pure, single race, or a hybrid species with archaic admixture. The various populations on earth, biologically speaking, do not behave like they are descended from a single ancestry. In the study of genetics, we find that blood factors transmit with much more exactitude than any other characteristic. If mankind evolved from the same African ancestors their blood would be compatible, but it is not.

For example, if not given special drugs to prevent complications, the pregnant body of a rhesus negative mother, impregnated by a rhesus positive man, will attack, and even try to fatally reject her own offspring. This form of allergic reaction can be fatal to the infant when the two different blood groups mingle, and it requires a blood transfusion to cure it.(62,63) The occurrence is common in the hybridization between different species in the animal kingdom, and will be covered in more detail in the next chapter.

Why does the body of an Rh negative mother carrying an Rh positive child reject her own offspring? Where did Rh negative blood group come from?

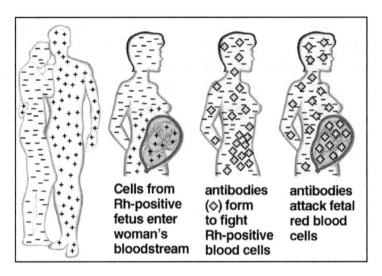

FIGURE 4

In 1937, Karl Landsteiner and Alexander S. Wiener discovered the RH blood factor. 85% of the human population has the Rh D antigen on their red blood cells which was in common with the Rhesus monkeys, while 15% of the population mysteriously do not have this antigen.(86) The 1994-2002 editions of Encyclopedia Britannica say that the Sweden County Dalarna today is characterized by almost pure Cro-Magnons:

Particularly noteworthy are the Dal people from Dalecarlia (now Dalarna, Sweden.) and the Guanches of the Canary Islands, the latter of which is said to represent a relatively pure Cro-Magnon stock.(86)

The Guanche is the name given to the original natives of the Canary Islands, who are now extinct, but they left behind tall mummies with blonde and red hair. Swedes fit a similar physical description. Genetics indicate that the RH negative factor originated in the blood of early Europeans at the time of Cro magnon, which we will explore in greater detail later. For now, it suffices to point out that Cro-magnon's DNA has remained unchanged in certain European populations for over 28,000 years.(98) Modern Northern Europeans are most similar to Cro magnon: tall, high frequency of RH negative blood type, fair haired and blue-eyed. It is interesting that blood from certain northern Europeans has successfully cured HIV.(95) Apparently, certain northern European populations have an immunity to HIV, so when receiving a bone marrow transplant an AIDS patient has been documented to no longer show signs of having HIV.(95)

Credo Mutwa, a well respected 94-year-old Zulu shaman, or "Sanusi", in South Africa, claims that native African tribes people had seen tall, blond, blue-eyed beings throughout the African continent many thousands of years before the white-skinned Europeans arrived. He said that when the Europeans first came, the black Africans thought they were the return of these same white "gods", whom they called the Mzungu. As a result they also called the European settlers by the same name. Credo's data, derived from ancient oral tradition, matches up quite nicely with the most recent genomic data concerning archaic admixture in Africa 35,000 years ago.(87) Native African genomes still contain signs of ancient mixing with other species (not present in non-African DNA).(88)

In 2011, the DNA from three African groups (Biaka Pygmies, San and Mandinka) was tested and shown to come from a now extinct species.(59) Researchers concluded that roughly 2% of the genetic material found in Sub-Saharan African populations came into their genome approximately 35,000 years ago from archaic hominins who had broken away from the modern human lineage around 700,000 years ago.(87)

In 2012, another study tested three sub-Saharan African populations (Pygmies, Hadza and Sandawe) and also found that the ancestors of modern Africans interbred with different species of hominins around 40,000 years ago; the same DNA is not found in the genomes of non-sub-Saharan Africans.(88) The median time of the most recent common ancestor of the African test subjects with the putative introgressive haplotypes was 1.2 – 1.3 million years ago. That means it was over 1 million years removed from not only modern humans, but also from anatomically correct humans in the fossil record.(88)

There are numerous other examples where two separate and distinct species from the same genus, often with a different numbers of chromosomes, can produce **viable** hybrid offspring. The domestic dog (Canis lupus familiaris) is a sub-species of the gray wolf (Canis lupus), and they produce viable hybrid offspring. Something on the order of 10 percent of North American birds, all considered specifically distinct, hybridize with other species.(74)

Blood Parrot hybrid: Cross breeding a Midas cichlid with a Red Devil cichlid

FIGURE 5

The blood parrot fish is a cichlid hybrid. It was created in Taiwan around 1986, and produced by cross breeding a Midas cichlid with a Redhead cichlid or a Red devil cichlid. Female blood parrots are usually fertile, whereas males are usually infertile, but there have been cases of successful breeding.(64)

Yakow hybrid: From crossbreeding a Yak with a domestic cow

FIGURE 6

The Yakow, or Dzo, is a hybrid that comes about from cross breeding a Yak with a domestic cow. The resulting animal is much larger than a cow or a yak, and is thought to produce much more milk and meat. All the females born from this cross are fertile, and they breed with either of the original species. The males born from this cross, however, are always infertile.(65)

Cama hybrid: From breeding a male Camel with a female Lama

FIGURE 7

The Cama results from breeding a male camel with a female lama. This animal was created to make something with the size and strength of a camel, but with the easier temperament and higher wool production of the lama. The Cama is quite small when born and doesn't have a hump. The cama are one of the few hybrids that is always fertile, however, as the lama is six times smaller and lighter than a camel, the only way to obtain a cama is by artificial insemination. Of course, you can also breed two of the fertile hybrid offspring together. (66)

Grolar hybrid: From a Grizzly bear mixed with a Polar bear

FIGURE 8

The grizzly-polar bear, or Grolar bear appears both in captivity and in the wild and there are reported sighting of these animals from as early as 1964. The grizzly-polar bear is a fertile hybrid, and there has even been a case of a second generation grizzly-polar bear, which was shot on Victoria Island. DNA tests established that the mother was a grizzly-polar bear and the father was a grizzly bear.(67)

Coywolf hybrid: From mixing a Wolf and a Coyote

FIGURE 9

The Coywolf, a coyote wolf hybrid, regularly occurs in nature. So regular, in fact, that all known red wolves have been found to have coyote genes in their lineage. This animal has caused a lot of problems for the Canid taxonomy, as hybrids are not usually referred to as a different species. Convention , however, would call the red wolf a sub species of the wolf, leaving its Latin name without any mention of its coyote genes. (68)

Savannah hybrid: Domestic cat mixed with a wild African Serval

FIGURE 10

The Savannah is a fairly modern domestic cat that was accepted as a new breed in 2001 by the International Cat Association. This cat is a hybrid of the domestic cat and the wild African Serval. Savannah's are a lot more social than most domestic cat breeds, and have often been compared to dogs because of their extreme loyalty. They are the highest jumpers, and the tallest cats in the cat world. How large and wild a savannah appears depends depends on what generation hybrid the savannah is. They often look very similar to a miniature version of a cheetah! (69)

Wholphin hybrid: From a Bottle-nose Dolphin and a Killer Whale

FIGURE 11

The Wholphin is an amazing "undersea" hybrid that comes from a bottle-nose dolphin having a successful pregnancy from a killer whale. The killer whale is not actually a whale, but a very large breed of dolphin. These remarkable wholphins have been known to occur in the wild, but so far there are only two living examples left in captivity.(70) A New York Times article titled, "Remarkable creatures", reported that:

The first captive wholphin, Kekaimalu, was born on May 15, 1985. The wholphin's size, color and shape are intermediate between the parent species. She has 66 teeth – intermediate between a bottle-nose (88 teeth) and false killer whale (44 teeth).(70)

Killer Bee: European bees mixed with Southern African bees

FIGURE 12

Killer bees, or Africanized honey bees, are man-made hybrid mistakes. They first came to being in 1957, when a replacement bee keeper accidentally released 26 Tanzanian queen bees in between the rest of the bee hives, on a farm in South Eastern Brazil. The hives had belonged to biologist, Warwick E. Kerr, who had intended to interbreed European bees with Southern African bees, to create a strain of bees that would produce more honey and adapt better to tropical conditions than European bees. Since their release, the killer bees have multiplied and migrated and can now be found throughout South America and through most of North America. Africanized honey bees are highly aggressive, hence the name killer bee, and move huge distances in massive swarms. When threatened in any way, they will attack in large numbers, ruthlessly stinging any threat to death, which happens to about two people a year in the US. (71)

Liger hybrid: From mixing an African Lion with a Bengal Tiger

FIGURE 13

The Liger is a hybrid between a male lion and a female tiger. Thus, both its parents are from the Panthera genus, but from different species. Ligers are the biggest of all the big cats, growing to almost the size of a lion and tiger combined. They carry characteristics from both parents; for instance their love of swimming from tigers and their highly social behavior from lions. Nowadays, ligers can only be found in captivity as their territories don't overlap. In history, however, there have been stories of ligers found in the wild. Ligers were long thought to be sterile, but in 1953, a liger success-fully mated with a male lion and the cub survived. (72)

An interesting study on hybridization between two species of modern-day howler monkeys in Mexico is shedding new light on why it has been difficult to trace, by analyzing fossil remains, the evidence of interbreeding among primates, and in particular ancient humans.(30) Researchers from the University of Michigan studied more than 200 adult howler monkeys (mantled howler monkeys and black howler monkeys) that they had captured and released in Mexico and Guatemala between 1998 and 2008. These two different species differ in appearance, differ in behavior, and differ in the number of chromosomes that each species possesses.(78) While both of the groups usually live in separate habitats, some of the howler monkeys in the Tabasco state of Mexico live in an overlapping, hybrid zone, where a minority population coexist and sometimes interbreed.

Mantled Howler monkeys and Black Howler monkeys

FIGURE 14

The research team collected blood samples, hair samples and morphometric measurements from the anesthetized animals for study before releasing them to their habitats again. Based on nuclear and mitochondrial DNA analysis, experts detected 128 hybrid individuals that were most likely the product of several years of interbreeding between hybrids and pure individuals. Statistical analysis on body measurements revealed many differences in the structure (morphology) of individual monkeys belonging to the mixed ancestry. (78) Researchers found that the individuals of mixed ancestry who shared most of their genome with one of the two species were physically indistinguishable from the pure individuals of that species. Liliana Cortés-Ortiz, from University of Michigan, said:

The implications of these results are that physical features are not always reliable for identifying individuals of hybrid ancestry. Therefore, it is possible that hybridization has been underestimated in the human fossil record. (78)

For years, researchers have attempted, using fossil records, to find evidence of interbreeding among human ancestral species. Mary Kelaita, now a postdoctoral fellow at the University of Texas at San Antonio, said that the study:

Suggests that the lack of strong evidence for hybridization in the fossil record does not negate the role it could have played in shaping early human lineage diversity.(30)

Recent sequencing of ancient genomes suggests that interracial cross-species interbreeding went on between the members of several ancient diverse groups more than 30,000 years ago, including an as-yet unknown human ancestor. "there were many hominid populations", according to Mark Thomas, evolutionary geneticist at University College London. (34)

Scientists recently sequenced a 37,000-year-old European genome, which allowed them to make some discoveries concerning Europe's earliest modern humans. The results show that present-day Scandinavians are the closest living relatives, genetically speaking, to the first Cro-magnon in Europe. The ancient genome also indicates that many European traits, including those from the Middle East, were already present in the first Europeans. The study, recently published in Science, sheds entirely new light on Europeans, which were originally a separate species from African lineages.(34)

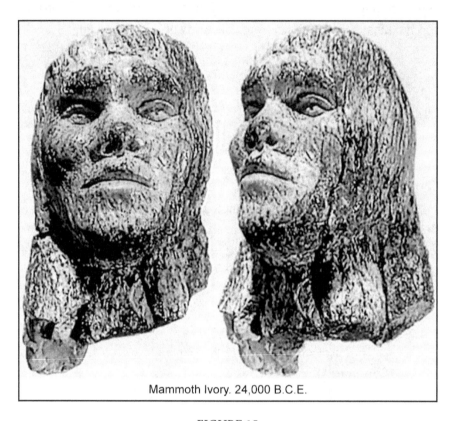

Mammoth Ivory. 24,000 B.C.E.

FIGURE 15

Chapter 3

C ro-Magnon first showed up in the fossil record just under 40,000 years ago, and officially lasted until about 10,000 years ago, roughly the start of the current Holocene age. This period is known as the Paleolithic Age in anthropology, commonly referred to as the ice age. The name "Cro-Magnon" derives from the "Abri de Cro Magnon" ("rock shelter" or "the big cave" in the local dialect) in southwest France, where the French geologist Louis Lartet found the first specimen in 1868.(43) Current scientific literature prefers the term "European Early Modern Humans" (or EEMH), instead of "Cro-Magnon". Anthropologist Richard C. Leonard writes:

An anthropological fact usually ignored in popular TV shows and documentaries is that there are notable differences between the Eastern and Western types of Upper Paleolithic man. In such shows the terms Cro-Magnon and Modern Man are used as if they were synonymous, whereas strictly speaking they are not. All Cro-Magnons are Modern, but all Moderns are not Cro-Magnon. Eastern European types are significantly different from "western"

Cro-Magnon Man, both physically and culturally. The "western" is known as Cro-Magnon, but the "eastern" are known by various other names, such as Brünn Man, Predmost, or Combe Capelle (wherever the remains were first found).(38)

◇◇

The eastern types were shorter in stature and almost always had less cranial capacity (a smaller brain) than the taller western Cro-Magnon types.(39) This is not meant as an insult or to suggest intelligence, but to point out that the western Cro-Magnon specimen was the tallest in the fossil record for this period, a fact often suppressed by academics in the mainstream. The female anatomy limits cranial size, and, for bipedals like humans, a larger head will always mean a taller being. Since bipedalism requires narrow hips, greater height (and thus larger hips) always comes with large skulls, such as that of Cro-Magnon. The height issue has been downplayed, or covered up altogether, since it does not neatly fit into a standard Darwinian notion, which supposes all of modern man's ancestors to be smaller ape-like creatures, not taller and bigger brained.

Indeed, Cro-Magnon's geographical distribution in Europe lies closest to the western part of Europe and North Africa, especially and probably most interestingly on a number of nearby Atlantic islands. The main museum in Las Palmas (Canary Islands, off the western African coast) claims to house the world's largest collection of Cro-Magnon skulls, as well as their well preserved mummies (more on this later). So what exactly is unique about Cro-Magnon vs other fossils of the same time period?(38) The various eastern European types are so similar that they are commonly lumped together as one by many mainstream anthropologists. The late Dr. Carleton S. Coon of Harvard University wrote:

◇◇

Despite the general homogeneity of Upper Paleolithic Man, these two groups, the western and the eastern, may be shown to have differed from each other in certain well-defined ways.(39)

◇◇

In other words, western Cro-Magnon Man differs from all the other types. The stone tool assemblage associated with these easterners is known as the Perigordian, and merely continues the earlier Neanderthal's tool-kit (the Mousterian) dating back hundreds of thousands of years, whereas the various Cro-Magnon tool assemblages were a totally new arrival.(79) According to French geologist and archaeologist Francois Bordes, Combe Capelle is not an invader bringing with him a Lower Perigordian culture:

The Perigordian tool industry did not come from elsewhere, but was only a continuation of the Mousterian tool industry of Nean-derthal Man. (40,79)

Around 35,000-40,000 years ago, suddenly something very new turned up in the archeological record, with a very different set of sophisticated stone tool technology. The Cro-magnon tool assemblage was labeled "Au-rignacian" and seemed to appear out of nowhere.(40) Prof. Bordes, the for-mer director of the Laboratory of Prehistory at the University of Bordeaux, explains:

The Aurignacian tool tradition - without doubt - originates outside of Europe, ready-made, although from where is still a mystery. (40)

Being the oldest known **modern** humans in Europe, the Cro-Magnon are linked to the well-known Lascaux cave paintings and the Aurignacian culture that flourished in western Europe by the Atlantic. They created the beautiful cave paintings found throughout the Pyrenees, and surrounding mountains, and which have become world famous.(79)

Chantal Jegues-Wolkiewiez is an independent researcher, astronomer and ethnologist with a PhD in Humanities. In November 2000 she presented a paper at the International Symposium of Prehistoric Art in Italy entitled: *Lascaux, the Magdalenians View of the Sky.* According to her studies, paleo-

Paleolithic cave art 30,000 BC

FIGURE 16

lithic (ice age) people spent long nights observing the sky, calculating, and recording their observations on the walls of caves.(97) The implications are staggering; the painters of Lascaux were astronomers, and ancient stargazers, who painted a zodiac on the walls of the cave, which showed the formation of the sky in the Magdalenian era, 17,000 years ago.(96)

These ancient star gazers, who lived 30,000 years before Zoroaster, payed especially close attention to the phases of the moon. They seemed to have linked the lunar cycle to the female ovulation cycle, based on the many fertility artifacts which appear to track the moon as it transitions from new to full. These same astronomical lunar markers can also be found painted in these caves. One example is this beautifully preserved deer, which has a row of dots ending in a square painted below it.

Another example appears under a brown horse, this time with 29 dots, one for each day of the month. It is thought to represent one lunar cycle, as the Moon phases through the sky.

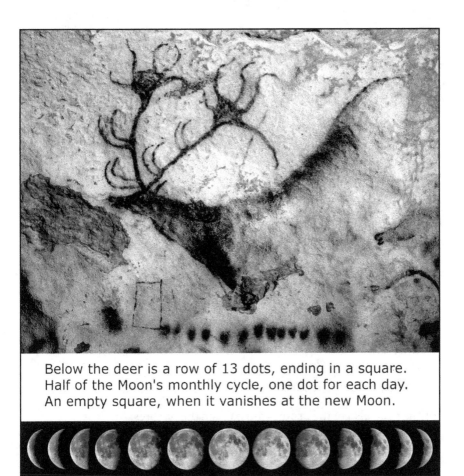

Below the deer is a row of 13 dots, ending in a square.
Half of the Moon's monthly cycle, one dot for each day.
An empty square, when it vanishes at the new Moon.

Different phases of the Moon.

FIGURE 26

Jegues-Wolkiewiez concludes in her research that the cave paintings recorded the constellations, fixed stars and the solstice points. She confirmed
her thesis by showing that all the constellations of the zodiac, except Aquarius and part of Pisces, are represented by the animals in their natural state of
that time.(96,97) The precision of the respective orientations as well as the
presence of the figure of the setting Sun demonstrates that Cro-Magnon descendants of the Magdalenian era were remarkable observers of the sky, and
were already using it to identify astrological cycles of time. This discovery of
ancient astronomy, if confirmed, could change our understanding of prehis-

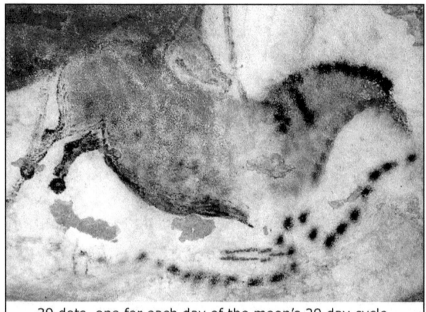

29 dots, one for each day of the moon's 29 day cycle

FIGURE 27

toric art and also of the people who painted the pictures. My personal take is that there is definitely astronomy on the walls of Lascaux.

The realization that Paleolithic people were great astronomers as well as extraordinary artists is revolutionary. The idea that they marked the zodiac belt as a band of sky that holds twelve constellations dancing in an eternal circle following the path of the Sun and that they painted these calculations on rock puts our understanding of the history of astronomy, and astrotheology, in a radically new light. This shows that in a far-off time people represented the actual constellations by drawing/tracing them on the pictures of certain animals particularly the bull. If true, they preceded the Babylonian astronomers by many thousands of years. As the ancient Mesopotamian, Greek, Phoenician, Minoan, and others also venerated the bull as an astrological symbol, this link becomes potentially all the more profound.

To explain the predominance of bulls in the prehistoric zodiac, Jegues-Wolkiewiez says that the constellation Taurus culminated in the Summer Solstice sky and was of primary importance to prehistoric painters.

The entire Hall of Bulls corresponds to the constellation Taurus. The eye of the Bull aligns with the super giant Aldebaran in the center of the constellation. A configuration of stars makes up the Hyades, which encircle the eye of Aldebaran. The Pleiades's are above his shoulder.(97)

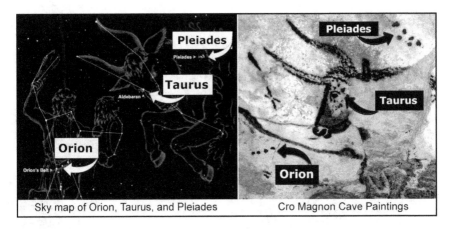

| Sky map of Orion, Taurus, and Pleiades | Cro Magnon Cave Paintings |

FIGURE 17

Further examples appear in the Facing Bulls who stand opposite each other. As pointed out by Jegues-Wolkiewiez, these bulls align with the constellations of Taurus and Scorpio.(97) That these constellations were not visible in the same sky at the time of the opposition strengthens her theory that Cro-Magnon people possessed a direct knowledge of astronomy.

Paleolithic cave art from 30,000 BC

FIGURE 18

At the end of the Axial Gallery is an animal unique to Lascaux, the upside down or Falling Horse. The legs and the head of this horse are visible in the passageway and raised towards the sky while the lower half of the body is hidden behind a fold of the wall. Jegues-Wolkiewiez measured the direction indicated by this horse and found it to be the point where the Sun rises on the first day of winter.(96)

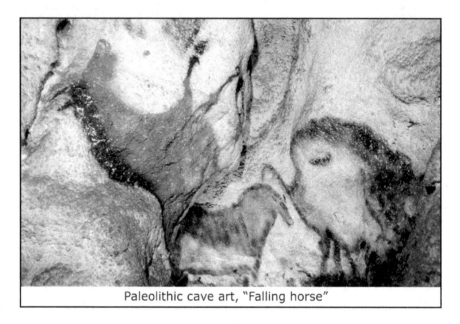

Paleolithic cave art, "Falling horse"

FIGURE 19

The presence above the Falling Horse of another horse, identical to the one in the main Hall of Bulls, strengthens the hypothesis giving Cro-magnon cave art astronomical significance. This second horse above the bulls corresponds to the constellations of Leo and Scorpio. This horse points to the brilliant star Arcturus and is exactly visible at the end of winter at the point above the horizon where the Sun rises. As the horse above, in profile, corresponds to the Sun at Spring Equinox, so below, the Falling Horse relates to the Sun at Winter Solstice.(96)

Art historians have long shown delight that the cave paintings are accurate in their knowledge of animal anatomy and the seasonal habits of each species. But what is important is that each painting in the Hall is aligned with a corresponding zodiac constellation. According to research conducted by Chantal Jegues-Wolkiewiez, it is the positions and relationships of the animals that indicate astronomical knowledge of the solstice positions, the constellations and the fixed stars. In other words, Cro-Magnon was not only an artist, but also astronomer and mathematician.

Crichton Miller argues that the Upper Paleolithic people originally created the cross as a mathematical device to help them understand astronomical cycles, by measuring the angular changes of the Earth and Moon by their spin and orbit. By measuring such changes based on the fixed signs of the Zodiac, the ancients were able to calculate time and thus, survive or even sail. Miller explains that Taurus the Bull was the first sign used to measure time:

The first sign used to predict the season was Taurus the Bull to represent the migration of the Auroch. The reflection of the Auroch as a symbol of time can be seen in wall paintings in Lascaux in France.(75)

This ties in well with Jegues-Wolkiewiez's work. There are certainly other artistic depictions as well. Some of the art depicts Cro-magnon wearing tailored clothes, hats, and they were clean-shaven in many cases. Bone needles and obsidian razors have been found, suggesting an advanced culture. Symbols scratched on bones record lunar and solar cycles and astrology. These were civilized people attempting to make the best of primitive, and possibly, post cataclysmic conditions.

One of the most important Cro-Magnon inventions was the needle. They made needles from slivers of animal bone, sharpened to a point at one end and with an eye at the other. With a needle, Cro-Magnon man could sew pieces of fur into better fitting garments. Evidence suggests that Cro-Magnon people developed close-fitting pants and shirts to protect them from the cold, as well as shawls, hoods, and long boots.

Jacquetta Hawkes, author of *The Atlas of Early Man*, believes that Cro-Magnon clothes approached those of modern Eskimos in their excellence of construction.(42) Cro-Magnon people often depicted those of

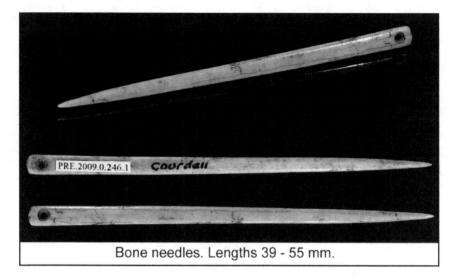

Bone needles. Lengths 39 - 55 mm.

FIGURE 20

their own kind with a sense of humor: many are caricatures, although a few examples are realistic, wearing bracelets and necklaces.(38) In fact, real jewelry begins at this time.(39,43)

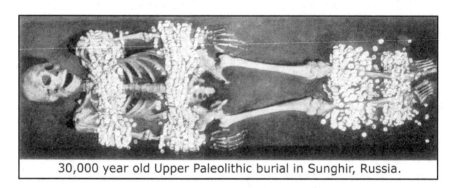

30,000 year old Upper Paleolithic burial in Sunghir, Russia.

FIGURE 21

Four stages of Cro-Magnon peoples appear in northern Africa, including the Canary islands, and fanning out from that western location. Anthropologists have also found four stages of remains/tools in the Azores and other Atlantic islands.(38) Anthropologist Richard C. Leonard calls these the "Atlantean Invasions", due to their apparent Atlantic origin, and proclaims:

◇◇

Near the date of 35,000 B.C., a taller, more powerfully built, more rugged man suddenly "invades" the western shores of Europe and North Africa (Bordes, 1968; Clark, 1970; Coon, 1954). This rugged, innovative, large-brained man is dubbed Cro-Magnon, named after the first specimen discovered at Cro-Magnon Cave a few miles from Aurignac; consequently, his tool assemblage was labeled Aurignacian.(38)

◇◇

The fossil record supports this statement. The Aurignacian was also the longest lasting of all Cro-Magnon cultures. Professor of anthropology at Rutgers University, Dr. John E. Pfeiffer, observes that the Aurignacian was quite distinct and that it arrived from some area outside of Western Europe; with an already "established way of life."(38) Pfeiffer observes that:

◇◇

The very coexistence of the Perigordians and Aurignacians in France raises some questions that cannot be answered at present. They apparently hunted in the same regions under the same conditions during the same general period, living as contemporaries for thousands of years. Yet they seem not to have influenced one another appreciably, a surprising state of affairs considering man's capacity for minding his neighbor's business. (41)

◇◇

Archeologist Frank Hibben states that although Aurignacian industry is found first in Western Europe, it is indubitably non-European in origin; adding that subsequent excavations and studies have shown that this tool kit is advanced and "far more complex than previously supposed."(38, 41) At about 18,000 B.C. the Aurignacian culture is "interrupted" by the next invasion of western Europe, known as the Solutrean. Only a few examples of Solutrean cave art are known. An example is the cave loci at Aragon and Levante (Spain). (38) However, the Solutreans excelled in the production of extremely delicate blades and they may also have introduced the use of the bow-and-arrow. (41)

Artifacts from the Ice Age site at Mezin in the Ukraine, are considered at least 12,000 years old, and the actual layer for the artifacts could be as old as 17,000 BC. The earliest known swastika inscribed figurines carved from mammoth ivory: an equal-arm cross, some having a serpent-symbol spiral attached to the tip of each arm.

Mammoth ivory bird figurine with swastika symbols. 13,000 BC

FIGURE 22

But after a mere four thousand years, around 14,000 B.C., the third and so-called Magdalenian invasion occurred, in which the harpoon first appeared.(38) These invasions, as Leonard calls them, are all associated with waves of Cro-Magnon occupation onto western Europe. No formative, or gestation, stages have ever been found on any continent for any of the Cro-Magnon tool industries. Where were they all developed? (38, 43) Leonard's vivid interpretation of the evidence continues:

The evidence tells of a powerful people who could live where they wanted to live... And there is more than that in the record. Life was changing in response to events which involved geological forces and caused a major population explosion. Surviving signs of the change are everywhere. The most recent Magdalenians occupied three to four times more sites than their predecessors, and occupied a large number of sites that had never been used before. (38)

⬦⬦⬦

Human populations were at a record high at this point; but something cataclysmic must have happened. The final Azilian "invasion" occurred very close to the magic date of 10,000 B.C., (compatible with the demise of Atlantis according to Plato) ending forever the Upper Paleolithic Age and the Cro-Magnon invasions. In fact, all Upper Paleolithic cultures - both eastern and western - ended at the same time, and many species became extinct. Geologically speaking, a new "age" began.(38) Archeologists and anthropologists the Mesolithic Age which followed as "gloomy," "uninspired."(38) It began with a significant drop in population (46). But even though the dreary Mesolithic Age had begun all over Europe, Africa and Asia, the Cro-Magnon based Azilian was unmistakably Upper Paleolithic in character for as long as it existed: yet all was not right with this last of the brilliant Cro-Magnon cultures. (38, 79)

What caused these sudden periodic migrations of people? Did people flee a violent catastrophe, such a volcano, or possibly the effects of rapidly rising sea levels during the end of the Pleistocene (ice age)? Anthropologists haven't the foggiest idea of the origin of these Cro-Magnon invasions.(79) They invariably appeared on the western shores of Europe and north Africa, including some of the Atlantic isles (Azores islands, Canary Islands). The settlement sites clustered in the west, with the number of sites diminishing towards the east.

This mystery has plagued anthropologists for over a hundred years. To the west, there is nothing but empty ocean: how could the invasions have come from there?

The mystery of these invasions has been so embarrassing that many anthropologists don't want to confront it directly. Some have gotten around the problem by blurring the distinction between true "Atlantic" Cro-Magnons and the "eastern" European types.(38) Calling all modern non-African men "Cro-Magnon", according to Leonard, merely skirts the issue.(38)

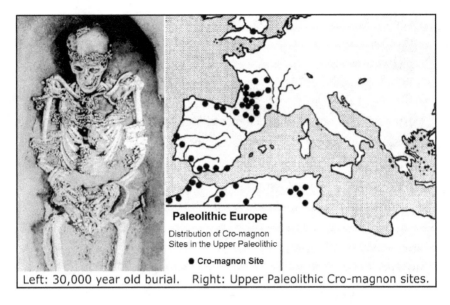

Left: 30,000 year old burial.   Right: Upper Paleolithic Cro-magnon sites.

FIGURE 23

It is not a scientific way to deal with the problem. In an article entitled, "Why don't We Call Them Cro-Magnon Anymore?", K. Krist Hirst suggests that the physical dimensions of Cro-Magnon specimens are not sufficiently different from modern humans to warrant a separate designation. Leonard raises the concern that this would make it all too convenient to eliminate the embarrassing origin problem. And what about the even more import-ant cultural differences (totally differing tool kits, settlement patterns, art impulse, etc.)?(38) Are we to simply "bland out" all these diversities under one designation? This doesn't strike me as a scientific practice. In 1994, Professor Goran Burenhult of Gotland University in Sweden elucidated:

Humans migrated into Europe about 40,000 years ago. They used two different tool traditions at this time. In North Africa and West-ern Europe, a new tool tradition started 35,000 years ago. These are associated with early Cro-Magnon cultures, called the Aterian culture.(77)

Cro-Magnon man has traditionally been called Atlantic because of his geographical distribution:

- Abbe' Breuil (1912) called the areas of Cro-Magnon occupation "Atlantic"
- Lundman (1977) used the term "Paleo-Atlantic" when referring to Cro-Magnon culture
- Prof. J. L. Myers (1923-1939) described Cro-Magnon culture as "a well-marked regional culture of the Atlantic coastal plain."

The "eastern" types of modern man may have originated in the Middle East, or Asia, eventually finding their ways into Europe when conditions there were favorable. These types were clearly wanderers, as indicated by their extremely thin and widely scattered occupation sites, more or less evenly distributed throughout Europe and the Middle East with no clustering toward the east or west.(76)

Cro-Magnon sites, on the other hand, are usually thick, indicating a long, settled occupation in one place. Their archeological sites cluster toward the western portions of Europe and Africa. The remains of structures indicate that both "eastern" and "western" Upper Paleolithic man commonly lived in houses of some sort, and not in caves as commonly assumed.(76) Many Cro-Magnon villages consisted of houses, but we don't know what they were made of. All we have are the remains of hearths and post hole patterns. They had spear throwers called "atlatl", harpoons, bows and arrows, arrow straighteners, obsidian razors, needles, musical instruments, even bone calendars carved with symbolic notations bordering on writing. (90) They domesticated several species of animals, a so-called "Neolithic" trait, which may have included the horse (76, 91, 92, 93). Numerous horse engravings include lines which look like bridles. This is strong evidence in favor of the domestication of the horse by Cro magnon.

A number of sites, dating back as far as 16,000 B.C, evidence the practice of agriculture. Archeologists, not knowing how to account for such a circumstance, labeled these activities a "false dawn"(94). Professional anthropologists realize that without agriculture, Atlantis, or any other antediluvian civilization, is no more than a myth. During the Magdalenian

Paleolithic engravings showing horses with straps and bridles

FIGURE 24

Period (16,000-10,000 B.C.) the innovations in technology came so fast that archeologists had to divide it up into Magdalenian I-VI. (76)

Some have speculated that the four "invasions" occurred simply because Atlantis was geologically unstable, and every few thousand years underwent serious upheavals, sending hordes of refugees onto several Atlantic islands and the western coasts of the continents of Europe and Africa (76). This brings up another mystery: Without Atlantis, how did these "boatless primitives" get scattered amongst the Canaries, the British Isles and others?

Ocean levels, were 400 feet lower than they are today during certain periods of the Ice Age, which left many of these islands connected to Europe by "land bridges". Many professionals speculate that ancient Cro-Magnon men used such land bridges to populate the islands from the mainland. But where is the evidence of the necessary "gestation period" for the advanced tool industries of Cro-Magnon Man? Absolutely no such evidence has ever been uncovered. As stated by Prof. Bordes, the Aurignacian arrived "ready-made" from "elsewhere", as did the Aterian in North Africa. (40)

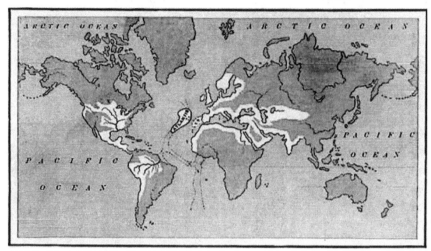

Map by Ignatius Donnelly placing Atlantis over the Azores Islands in the North Atlantic Ocean.

FIGURE 25

The final "invasion," the Azilian, occurred approximately 10,000 B.C., suspiciously close to the date Plato says Atlantis sank. We have four Cro-Magnon invasions, on both sides of Gibraltar, occurring over a period of just under 25,000 years: the Aurignacian, Solutrean, Magdalenian and Azilian. The last one occurred just when Atlantis was said to have sub-sided, and since that magic date, there have been no more Cro-Magnon invasions. Atlantis, the apparent source of the invasions, was gone. (40, 76)

Cro-Magnon had a very tall stature. He averaged well over six feet, and sported rather heavy cheek bones, a heavy brow and a strong jaw. The original race of Cro-Magnon was extremely dolichocephalic (long-headed from front to back) and yet had a short face and large forehead. This odd combination is known among anthropologists as "disharmonism," who considered it a diagnostic (or defining) trait of Cro-Magnon.(43) His brain was so large that even with the large jaw and prominent chin, his forehead-to-chin line is basically vertical. Where Combe Capelle and Brünn Man averaged an above average 1525cc. (41), a Cro-Magnon specimen's brain case was measured at 1743cc. (76). Cro-Magnon types have also been found in certain portions of North and South America, even as far south as Tierra del Fuego where 10,000-12,000 year-old Cro-Magnon-type skeletons have been found.(76) These distinctions assume greater importance if Atlantis is the possible source of the first humans that are modern, and not just anatomically correct.

So we have a unique fossil specimen found in both western Europe, and on the other side of the Atlantic. Could Cro-Magnon Man really be Atlantean? One thing is for certain, nothing in the fossil or genetic record that indicates that he originated in sub-Saharan Africa; a theory that may still be politically correct, but can no longer be considered scientifically correct.

Chapter 4

When looking at the British Isles on a map, their slight size may make some of us wonder if thousands of years from today, will people still suppose that a small group of islands might have established trade routes that connected the cultures of the civilized world? Will the British Empire eventually be set aside as just another old-fashioned myth? In 1882, Congressman Ignatius Donnelly remarked:

> There are in Plato's narrative no marvels; no myths, It is a plain and reasonable history of a people who built temples, ships, and canals; who lived by agriculture and commerce; who, in pursuit of trade, reached out to all the countries around them.. We see an immigrant enter the country, marry one of the native women, and settle down; in time a great nation grows up around him.(101)

In other words, it was just as normal for Donnelly to accept the likelihood of a non-fictional Atlantean history as described by Plato, as it was

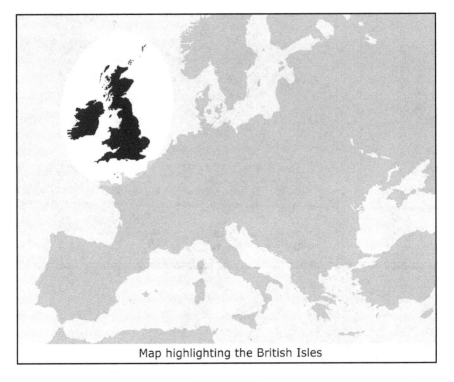

Map highlighting the British Isles

FIGURE 28

to suppose that a great network of English-speaking governments should grow up around the small British Isles: exploring, trading, colonizing. Plato was perhaps not reporting a departed sea myth, but an overlooked or forgotten geopolitical domain of an antediluvian sea-faring people governing over a maritime civilization. (131)

Plato's account of Atlantis comes to us through two of his books, *Timaeus* and *Critias*. The narrative is passed down through a conversation told to him by his distinguished grandfather Solon, who traveled to Egypt and brought back to Athens the ancient Egyptian legend. The Egyptian priests respected Solon's status and reputation and cordially welcomed him. They also respected the ancient Athenians, whom they regarded as kinsmen, believing their deity Neith to be the same deity that the Greeks knew as Athena. Both Sais (Egypt) in 8,600BC, and Athens (Greece) in 9,600BC, were said to have been founded by the same patron Goddess Athena (Neith).(102,138)

Solon was a highly regarded Greek statesman, renowned for his poetry, social reforms, and semi-egalitarian politics; most notably wealth distribution. Today, statues of Solon are displayed in the halls of the Library of Congress, US House of Representatives, and the Supreme Court of the United States, honoring the contributions that Solon made to reforming and creating egalitarian laws and initiating the formation of democratic government as opposed to rule exclusively by a nobility.(139)

Solon is known to have had traveled to Sais, Egypt, in 560 BC and learned the Atlantean tale from a group of priests: legends which they obtained from very ancient tablets and writings on columns inscribed within Egypt's most royal chambers. Atlantis was finally destroyed around 9650 BC, according to the royal inscriptions.(140)

Ancient Egyptian Tomb Hieroglyphics

FIGURE 29

The priests said that Atlantis was located outside of the Pillars of Hercules, which was what the rocks of Gibraltar were known as in ancient times. This puts Atlantis somewhere in the Atlantic, which one could assume to be the name of the ocean surrounding Atlantis.(102,138) We learn from the Egyptian priests that the ocean conditions were different in the antediluvian past, which makes sense as sea levels globally were 400 feet lower during the ice age, when Atlantis was said to have existed, than they are today. Small islands in the Atlantic, such as the Azores, would have been connected and had much more dry surface area. The priests continue:

In those far-away days that Ocean could be navigated, as there was an island outside the channel which your countrymen tell me you call the 'pillars of Heracles'. This island was larger than Libya and Asia together, and from it seafarers, in those times, could make their way to the others, and thence to the whole opposite continent, which encircles the true outer Ocean.(138)

The Egyptian priest who spoke to Solon was impressed with the ancient, yet advanced, sea-faring civilization of the Atlanteans. This is worth mentioning because in those distant times, even though in decline for centuries, Egypt was thought to be the most advanced civilization in the world at the time.(138)

The priest mentioned that the Atlanteans were in possession of a very advanced technology. He also claimed that the Atlanteans did not fear death. Either they believed themselves to be immortal or they knew enough about the afterlife not to be afraid of dying. The priests told Solon the magnificent ancient civilization disappeared roughly 9,000 years before his time in 500 B.C.. He went on to explain to Solon why it was that the Egyptians still retain their ancient records and why the Greeks do not: as a direct consequence of the many global catastrophes that had befallen them, which periodically knocked their civilization back into a primitive state of collective amnesia.(138) The Egyptian priest continued to explain:

Whereas just when you and other nations are beginning to be provided with letters and the other requisites of civilized life, after the usual interval, the stream from heaven, like a pestilence, comes pouring down, and leaves only those of you who are destitute of letters and education; and so you have to begin all over again like children, and know nothing of what happened in ancient times, either among us or among yourselves. There have been, and will be again, many destructions of mankind arising out of many causes; the greatest have been brought about by the agencies of fire and water, a declination of the bodies moving in the heavens around the earth, and a great conflagration of things upon the earth, which recurs after long intervals. You remember a single deluge only, but there were many previous ones; in the next place, you do not know that there formerly dwelt in your land the fairest and noblest race of men which ever lived, and that you and your whole city are de-scended from a small seed or remnant of them which survived. And this was unknown to you, because, for many generations, the survivors of that destruction died, leaving no written word.(138)

Solon diligently translated the historical records to take back to Athens, from Egyptian into the Greek language, vividly depicting the amazing events being described to him and expertly deciphering the names of the characters in this ancient epic saga. Plato continues to describe the ancient empire as Solon had dictated it millenia ago:

Solon marveled at his words, and earnestly requested the priests to inform him exactly and in order about these former citizens. You are welcome to hear about them, Solon, said the priest, both for your own sake and for that of your city, and above all, for the sake of the goddess who is the common patron and parent and educator of both our cities. She founded your city a thousand years before ours, receiving from the Earth and Hephaestus the seed of your race, and afterwards she founded ours, of which the constitution is recorded in our sacred registers to be eight thousand years old. Now in this island of Atlantis there was a great and wonderful empire which had rule over the whole island and several others, and over parts of the continent, and, furthermore, the men of Atlantis had subjected the parts of Libya (modern day Africa) within the columns of Heracles as far as Egypt, and of Europe as far as Tyrrhenia (modern day Italy). This vast power, gathered into one, endeavored to subdue at a blow our country and yours and the whole of the region within the straits; and then, Solon, your country shone forth, in the excellence of her virtue and strength, among all mankind. She was preeminent in courage and military skill, and was the leader of the Hellenes. And when the rest fell off from her, being compelled to stand alone, after having undergone the very extremity of danger, she defeated and triumphed over the invaders, and preserved from slavery those who were not yet subjugated, and generously liberated all the rest of us who dwell within the pillars.(138)

The description of how the Atlantean civilization came about, as given by Plato in the *Critias*, can be summarized by interactions between an elite bloodline of people who are the "gods" and the mortals that they governed. In the first ages the gods divided the earth among themselves, proportioning it according to their respective dignities. Each became the peculiar deity of his own allotment and established magnificent temples to himself, ordained a priest-craft, and instituted a system of sacrifice.(138) To Poseidon was given the sea and the island continent of Atlantis. In the midst of the island was a mountain which was the dwelling place of Cleito, a primitive mortal human being. The maiden was very beautiful, she soon was wooed by Poseidon, who then had children by her. (138)

Poseidon apportioned his continent among these children, and Atlas, the eldest son, he made overlord. Poseidon further called the country Atlantis and the surrounding sea the Atlantic in honor of Atlas. Plato goes on to say:

The descendants of Atlas continued as rulers of Atlantis, and with wise government and industry elevated the country to a position of surpassing dignity. The natural resources of Atlantis were apparently limitless. Precious metals were mined, wild animals domesticated, and perfumes distilled from its fragrant flowers. While enjoying the abundance natural to their semi-tropic location, the Atlanteans employed themselves also in the erection of palaces, temples, and docks. They bridged the zones of sea and later dug a deep canal to connect the outer ocean with the central island, where stood the palaces. And temple of Poseidon, which excelled all other structures in magnificence. A network of bridges and canals was created by the Atlanteans to unite the various parts of their kingdom. (138)

◇◇

Plato then describes the white, black, and red stones which they quarried from beneath their continent and used in the construction of public buildings and docks.

◇◇

The citadel, on the central island, contained the palaces, temples, and other public buildings. In its center, surrounded by a wall of gold, was a sanctuary dedicated to Cleito and Poseidon. Here the first ten princes of the island were born and here each year their descendants brought offerings. Poseidon's own temple, its exterior entirely covered with silver and its pinnacles with gold, also stood within the citadel. The interior of the temple was of ivory, gold, silver, and orichalch, even to the pillars and floor. The temple contained a colossal statue of Poseidon standing in a chariot drawn by six winged horses, about him a hundred Nereids riding on dolphins. Arranged outside the building were golden statues of the first ten kings and their wives. In the groves and gardens were hot and cold springs. There were numerous temples to various deities, places of exercise for men and for beasts, public baths, and a great race course for horses. At various vantage points on the zones were fortifications, and to the great harbor came vessels from every maritime nation. The zones were so thickly populated that the sound of human voices was ever in the air. That part of Atlantis facing the sea was described as lofty and precipitous, but about the central city was a plain sheltered by mountains renowned for their size, number, and beauty. The plain yielded two crops each year, in the winter being watered by rains and in the summer by immense irrigation canals, which were also used for transportation. The plain was divided into sections, and in time of war each section supplied its quota of fighting men and chariots. Each of the kings of Atlantis had complete control over his own kingdom, but their mutual relationships were governed by a code engraved by the first ten kings on a column' standing in the temple of Poseidon.(138)

Plato concludes his description by declaring that it was this great empire which attacked the Hellenic states. This did not occur, however, until their power and glory had lured the Atlantean kings from the pathway of wisdom and virtue. Filled with false ambition, the rulers of Atlantis determined to lustfully conquer the entire world. Zeus, perceiving the wickedness of the Atlanteans, gathered the gods into his holy habitation and addressed them. Here Plato's narrative comes to an abrupt end, for the Critias was never finished.(138) In his other writing that mentions Atlantis, *Timaeus, there* is a further description of the violent end to their civilization given to Solon by the Egyptian priest, which concludes:

But afterwards there occurred violent earthquakes and floods; and in a single day and night all your warlike men in a body sank into the earth, and the island of Atlantis in like manner disappeared, and was sunk beneath the sea. And that is the reason why the sea in those parts is impassable and impenetrable, because there is such a quantity of shallow mud in the way; and this was caused by the subsidence of the island.(102)

These conditions are a fair description of the transition time from the date Plato gives for the demise of Atlantis around 9500BC. Global sea levels have risen 300-400 feet since the ice age, when Plato's Atlantis was said to have existed, so submerged islands in the Atlantic makes sense.

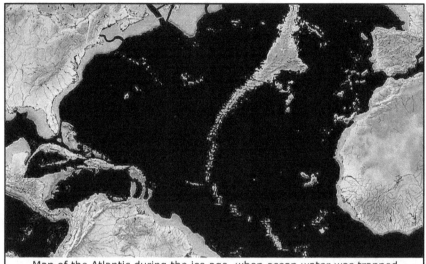

Map of the Atlantic during the ice age, when ocean water was trapped as glaciers, and sea levels were 400 feet lower than they are today.

FIGURE 30

There were mass extinctions world wide. Volcanic activity was considerably higher than it is today, enough for scientists to end two geological ages (Pliocene and Pleistocene) right at Plato's date for the demise of Atlantis, and start a new one (Holocene) after 1.8 million years.

The ancient Egyptian word for Atlantis is Aten or Atlen. Many ancient peoples give remarkably similar names to an island or continent formerly situated in the Atlantic Ocean. The Berber tribes of North Africa call it Attala, the Basques of the Pyrenees call it Atlaintika, the northern European Vikings call it Atli, the Mesopotamian Babylonians call it Arallu, and the Mesoamerican Aztecs called it Aztlan or Tulan. The Hindus referred to Atlantis in various stages of its evolution, as Atala, Saka-dvipa (early Atlantis), Sveta-dvipa ('white island'), Ruta and Daitya (large remaining islands after most of Atlantis had sunk), and Sankha- (or Sancha-) dvipa (Poseidonis). (105)

Plato's interpretations propose that Atlantis was a global diffusion. That it's legend and mythologies had reached all corners of the world in undeniable. This is made clear by the sacred god-king lists around the world, documenting the procession of not only the earliest deities of history, but their demigod progeny as well.(103) Atlantis is described by Plato as being ruled by ten kings before its demise. This same list of ten rulers, comes down to us in all ancient works referring to antediluvian, pre-flood times, including the Bible and Sumerian King list. Egyptian mythology also states that there were originally 10 antediluvian god-kings, who ruled in a foreign country to the West. They were called Au-riteans, but the actual pronunciation is unsure because hieroglyphs only approximate audible real sounds.(104) Sanchuniathon, the great Phoeni-cian historian, calls the same kings "Aleteans" in 1193 BC which is 600 years before Plato was even born, so it predates Plato, Herodotus, and even Solon. (133)

The Egyptian Book of the Dead which is believed to be composed around 4000 BC, tells of an Island in the West which was destroyed by water, and the surviving god-kings sailed eastward to Egypt.(134) These same god-kings could easily be compared to the Titans in Greek mythol-ogy and are indeed one and the same. The ancient Egyptians, Sumerians, and Greeks not only referred to the 10 god-kings, but also list their replace-ments, which occurred at approximately 9850 BC.

Manetho, also known as Manethon of Sebennytos, was an Egyptian historian and priest from Sebennytos who lived during the Ptolemaic era, circa 3rd century BC. He recorded *Aegyptiaca* (History of Egypt), and his historic contributions are of great interest to Egyptology, and are often used as evidence for the chronology of the reigns of pharaohs. Manetho trans-lated the Egyptian king lists in 250 BC, and reveals that the total number of years covered by all the king-lists equals 36,525. This time frame perfectly matches the period of Cro-Magnon man in the fossil record.(135,136) Ac-cording to the chronology of Manetho, about 36,525 years ago Gods on Earth began to rule Earth, ruling until about 22,625 years ago when Demi-gods succeeded them, ruling until about 11,600 years ago Mortal Humans began to rule Earth, ruling up to the present day. (136) He also points out that the FIRST kings did not rule from Egypt, but a foreign country. Egypt was originally either an outpost, colony, or conquered nation.(104) In the Bible (Genesis 6:1-2,4), is says:

And it came to pass, when men began to multiply on the face of the earth, and daughters were born unto them, that the sons of God saw the daughters of men that they were fair; and they took them wives of all which they chose. There were giants in the earth in those days; and also after that, when the sons of God came in unto the daughter of men, and they bare children to them, the same became mighty men which were of old, men of renown.(137)

Other direct sources are the king-list in the temple of Osiris at Abydos, the Palermo Stone (a Fifth Dynasty document) and the Turin Papyrus (a 19th Dynasty document).(104,136) King Thoth, often called Thoth the Atlantean or the Scribe, is credited with inventing writing and much of his writings can be found in the Egyptian Book of the Dead. He supposedly lived as a noble ruler on an "Island of Flame to the West".(104) Plato describes the Atlanteans as being a noble race in the beginning, but becoming greedy, materialistic, warlike, and genetically diluted by mixing sexually with "mortals". In *Critias* (360BC), Plato writes:

For many generations, as long as the divine nature lasted in them, they were obedient to the laws, and well-affectioned towards the god, whose seed they were; for they possessed true and in every way great spirits.(138)

However, the Atlanteans disobeyed their cultural and social taboos regarding interracial mixing, and according to the Egyptians, via the Greeks, their once great civilization and empire became debased and corrupt:

> When the divine portion began to fade away, and became diluted too often and too much with the mortal admixture, and the human nature got the upper hand, they then, being unable to bear their fortune, behaved unseemly, and to him who had an eye to see grew visibly debased.(138)

According to Plato, the Atlanteans inherited their "god-like" appearances from Poseidon, who fell in love with Cleito and built her a palace in Atlantis on a hill. They had 5 sets of twins, for which the eldest was called Atlas, and thus the name of not only the island/continent, but also a specific star in the Pleiades from which they claim to have descended from. (102,138)

THE PEOPLING OF THE AMERICAS

The Clovis culture is a prehistoric paleo-Indian culture that appears 11,500 RCYBP (radiocarbon years before present), at the end of the last glacial period (ice age), characterized by the manufacture of "Clovis points" (spear tips) and distinctive bone and ivory tools.

According to the 'Clovis first' paradigm, which gained ascendancy in the mid-20th century, the first inhabitants of the Americas were people associated with the Clovis culture. Beginning somewhere around 12,000 BC, they theoretically crossed from Siberia to Alaska over the Beringia land bridge created by the lower sea levels during the ice age, and advanced southwards via an ice-free corridor east of the Rocky Mountains as the glaciers retreated. They then quickly spread to all parts of the America and supposedly populated all of South America.

Before the second world war, mainstream anthropologists insisted that humans first entered America only 4000 years ago, and anyone arguing otherwise was treated with hostility. Once the evidence for habitation by the Clovis culture as early as 12,000 BC became widely accepted, they then proceeded to treat any professionals claiming to have found evidence of an even earlier human presence in the Americas with the same prejudice that they themselves had previously suffered. Nevertheless, the Clovis-first paradigm became increasingly untenable as reliable evidence mounted of earlier human habitation.

Many researchers doubt that Native Americans had a single cultural origin, as they spoke an incredible variety of languages, held a multitude of religious beliefs and customs, and practiced a host of different and often contrasting lifestyles.

The resemblance of many modern Native Americans to the Mongoloid peoples of Asia was recognized long ago, and migrations from that region have likely taken place. However, only at specific times did Beringia form an ice-free land bridge and was there an ice-free corridor into the heart of North America. This is one of the reasons why the possibility of coastal/maritime migration is also widely recognized. The fixation on migrations via the Bering Strait is scientifically unjustified. The earliest archaeological sites are not found in eastern Beringia, nor do sites get progressively younger as one travels south through the Americas.

Using modern genetic analysis, scientists have discovered that Northern European people including some British, Scandinavians, French, and some Eastern Europeans descend from a mixture of two very different ancestral populations, and one of these groups is related to Native Americans. This research was published in the November 2012 issue of the Genetics Society of America's journal Genetics. According to Nick Patterson, first author of the report:

There is a genetic link between the paleolithic population of Europe and modern Native Americans. The evidence is that the population that crossed into the Americas more than 15,000 years ago was likely related to the ancient population of Europe.(108)

Whoever the Clovis people were, they hunted large game and left behind distinct spear points that were found over much of North and Central America in the early 20th century. Nothing similar has been found in Eastern Asia, Siberia, or Beringia. Clovis points resemble spear points of the Cro-Magnon or the following Solutrean culture, which was dominant in present-day France and Spain from about 21,000 to 17,000 years ago. According to George Weber, author of "Clovis People":

It is significant that the oldest Clovis tools are being found in the eastern and southeastern regions of North America, rather than in the northwest, where one would expect them if the Clovis people came from Siberia and Alaska. (106)

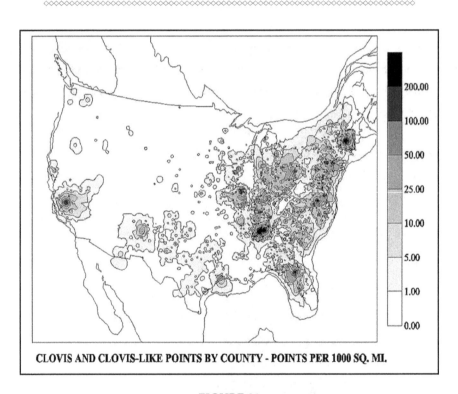

CLOVIS AND CLOVIS-LIKE POINTS BY COUNTY - POINTS PER 1000 SQ. MI.

FIGURE 31

Dr. Douglas W. Owsley, the Division Head of Physical Anthropology for the National Museum of Natural History at the Smithsonian Institution, has recently described the 9,500 year old Kennewick skull, as well as certain other ice age American skulls dated to over 9,000 years old, as being "long-headed and having a short face."(107) Dr. Göran Burenhult, professor of archeology at Gotland University in Sweden comments:

On ancient Caucasians in America, Kennewick man, has not been the only find. Others include the 13,000 year old Peñon skull found in Mexico, the 12,500 year old Monte Verde site in Chile, the 9,400 year old Spirit Cave Mummy in Churchill County, Nevada, and others. DNA distinguishing U.S. Indians from Mongoloids also strengthens the above evidence. Pre-Clovis and Clovis stone tools found in America are similar to those in North Western Europe known as Solutrean. Such tools have never been found in Siberia. (107)

Stone tools found at Cactus Hill in Virginia, dated to 17,000-15,000 BP, seem to represent a transitional style between the Solutrean and Clovis cultures. Similar sites include Page-Ladson in Florida, with animal bones and human artifacts reaching back to about 14,500-12,500 BP, and the Meadowcroft rock shelter in southwestern Pennsylvania, with evidence of occupancy dating to 19,000-16,000 BP. (106) A growing number of archeologists insist that people associated with the Solutrean culture must have migrated from Europe to North America around 20,000 to 15,000 BP, when their stone-tool technology later influenced the development of the Clovis toolmaking culture in the Americas.

RED PAINT PEOPLE: THE MARITIME ARCHAIC

Thousands of years before Columbus and Eric the Red, a tall, fair skinned people lived in well organized communities on the coasts of Brittany, Denmark, Labrador, and especially Maine. Biological traits in the skulls and skeletons of the Maritime Archaic, as they are called, indicate they are of the same racial make up as some of the Basque people of Europe.(109) Although dating all the way back to 7000 BC, these people had developed a high degree of craftsmanship, expertly using fire-making tools of a sort superior to those of the later Indians. Their implements imply a high degree of skill in woodworking, and they made boats in which they seem to have traveled considerable distances. (107)

They are more famously referred to as the "Red paint people" due to their traditional use of red ochre painted onto their skin, where we get the term "red skins". Of course, its made derogatory for political reasons which has nothing to do with ethnicity, since these Natives from that time period were as white-skinned as the Basque in Spain. The Red paint people also used red ochre heavily for rituals, sprinkling it all across their graves and the deceased relatives. This is a well established burial custom that can be seen wherever Cro magnon types have settled, including the other side of the Atlantic. An example would be in Egypt, where the oldest remains belonging to a naturally mummified red-head 5,500 years ago nicknamed "Ginger", on display at the British museum.

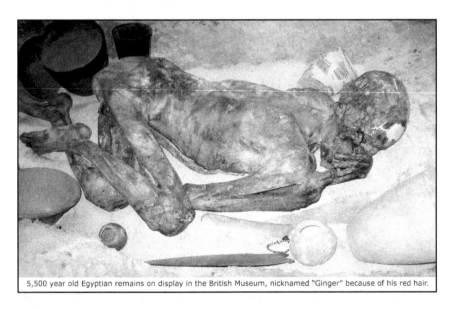

5,500 year old Egyptian remains on display in the British Museum, nicknamed "Ginger" because of his red hair.

FIGURE 32

The same can still be seen on the ancient Egyptian walls and statues, the men symbolically painted red. Symbolism aside, red ochre is composed of iron oxide, which is the active ingredient in most brands of sunscreen; a must for any ultra fair skinned people in regions that require protection from the sun.

Since the time of the European settlements following the "discovery" made by Columbus, multitudes of red ochre graves have been found. Early New Englanders regarded them with extreme suspicion; to find one was considered an evil omen. Hardy adventurers, however, unearthing the paint, put it to good advantage when they saw that it gave a satisfactory finish to their furniture and other woodwork.

At first the ochre deposits, always accompanied as they were by strange stone weapons, were not imagined to be associated with burials. In the late nineteenth century, Dr. Augustus C. Hamlin of Bangor interested archeologists at Harvard University's Peabody Museum in investigating the Maine Red Paint cemeteries. Some of the best collections of Red Paint artifacts are at the Peabody Museum and at Phillips Andover Academy. The findings in about thirty Red Paint cemeteries have been recorded. (148)

Of course, many other cemeteries have been found of which there is no record, the relics having been dug out and lost or scattered. All the documented cemeteries in Maine are near water navigable for small boats. All but two are on stream banks or near the coast; the two exceptions, although on high ground, lie beside what may once have been the course of a stream now deflected in another direction.

The Red Paint people retained many traits and skills of their ancestors who escaped from Atlantis. However, just like other descendents and survivors around the world, their civilizations never reached the heights previously attained in their original homeland.

HAPLOGROUP X

What is mitochondrial DNA? Each mitochondrion (plural is mitochondria) is a separate bacteria. Each of our cells (except blood cells) contains hundreds to many thousands of mitochondria. The mitochondria convert sugar in the form of a glucose molecule, into energy. As such, the mitochondria are the basis of life, because without them many of our cells simply would not function. Since they are a separate bacteria, they have their own DNA that differs from human DNA. The mitochondrial DNA ladder has only 16,569 steps. Therefore it is much more conducive to use in research than is human DNA. It is abbreviated as mtDNA. Since the DNA of a mitochondion is not human, where does it come from when a new human is born? The answer is that the newly born child has taken some mitochondria from the mother - not the father. (139)

Now things get interesting. The DNA of the mitochondria mutate. They mutate at a well understood and predictable rate. By analyzing the mtDNA of living humans and comparing it to other humans, scientists can determine the lineage of the maternal line; from mothers to daughters. They can then take ancient samples of mtDNA, say from a tooth or bone that is thousands of years old, and begin to study ancient migration patterns. In some cases this analysis of mtDNA conflicts with the standing paradigms of archeology. Very noticeably this has occurred concerning the origin of American Indians. (139,141)

Since mtDNA mutates at a certain predictable rate, it's possible to judge when distant populations originally diverged, based on how different the mtDNA they have today is. If a group of people splits up, say some going east and some going west, mtDNA mutations found in the east but not the west likely originated after the group diverged. Count up the mutations and the rate at which they would have occurred and you can figure out an estimate for when the family tree branched off. (139)

"You literally have a genetic clock," explained Douglas Wallace, a professor of molecular medicine at the University of California, Irvine. Scientists categorize mtDNA into a number of so-called haplogroups, based on their similarities and differences. Professor Wallace simplifies things for us: "You can think of them as like blood types; they don't affect the way you live, but can be identified at the molecular level."(139)

The conventional wisdom to explain the peopling of the Americas is that migrants crossed from northeast Asia to Alaska around 12,000 years ago to become the ancestors of today's Native Americans. But mtDNA analysis has revealed some unexpected links between Europe and North America. When scientists analyzed the mtDNA of a broad sample of living Native Americans, they found that about 97 percent had mtDNA from haplogroups A, B, C or D. These haplogroups are all present in modern day Siberia and Asia, so it makes sense that the forefathers of those Native Americans came from those regions. But the surprise was that about 3 percent of the Native Americans tested had mtDNA from a different haplogroup, called X. Some populations, such as the Ojibwa from the Great Lakes region, have a high concentration of X (around 25 percent). (141)

It has recently been admitted by some geneticists that the founders of Native America included those of Caucasoid ancestry and that the presence of Haplogroup X in North America opens up the possibility of an early migration westward from Europe.(110,141)

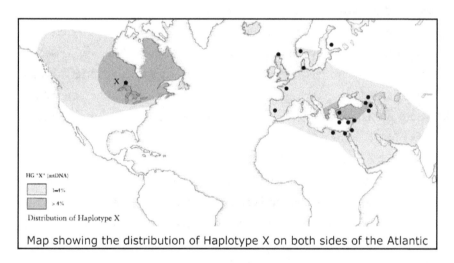

Map showing the distribution of Haplotype X on both sides of the Atlantic

FIGURE 33

Exactly how did haplogroup X get to North America? A small amount has been found near China's Tarim Basin (famous for it's ancient Caucasian mummies), but it's definitely not common in modern Asians. It can, however, be found in a substantial percent of the present day European population.(141)

By looking at the various mutations within haplogroup X, scientists are able to use that "genetic clock" to estimate when those early Europeans would have arrived. Depending on how large a group they assume headed west, they come up with two time ranges: either between 36,000 and 23,000 years ago or between 17,000 and 12,000 years ago.

Haplogroup X definitely did **not** arrive in America with the European explorers of the last 500 years, nor did it arrive with Eric the Red and the Vikings. European X and American X are different enough that scientists say they must have diverged tens of thousands of years ago, long before the age of exploration introduced European genes to the New World.(111) The evidence that Haplogroup X is not the result of Viking or even more recent European admixture would be its presence in ancient Native Americans. Ancient DNA samples from the Norris Farms site (149), the Windover site (150), and the Amazon Basin (151) exhibit the characteristic genetic markers found in individuals assigned to Haplogroup X. (112)

The evidence from mitochondrial DNA, passed on by mothers only, is supplemented by evidence from Y-chromosomes, which are passed on by fathers only. Native American Y-chromosomes show a variety of haplogroups, including haplogroups 4 and 1C, which are also characteristic of certain populations of Jewish peoples (142,143). Haplogroup 1C is common enough in the New World that it has been proposed as a major founder haplogroup for the New World. " (113)

In a 2001 study Haplogroup X was identified in ancient remains around 8,000 years old found in several cemeteries in the traditional area occupied by the Basque, the Pyrenees Mountains of France and Spain (also the location of the Cro magnon cave paintings). (114) Once the rare and mysterious haplogroup X was shown to be in the Basque population as well as in North America - the scales of evidence tipped in a new direction. The mitochondrial DNA discoveries show that the Basque population is related to the North American Indian population. Since these results were obtained from 6,000 to 8000 year old cemeteries in the Basque area and since they were also ancient in North America, they were not caused by activities occurring after Columbus. Instead they reveal an ancient connection. (115)

The time estimates on haplogroup X entering America were at first shaky, because too few samples had been taken. But later, it seemed hat Haplogroup X entered by 28,000 B.C. and again in 10,000 B.C. These appear to be waves of immigration from the Atlantic. The second wave corresponds to the date of the sinking of Atlantis as given by Plato. That should count as another supportive discovery. The common origin of both European and American paleolithic culture from the ancient civilization of Atlantis makes total sense as one continues to ponder the multitude of similarities, especially genetically and culturally.

One may ask then why then is there not a greater degree of visible Caucasian racial types evident in America today? The answer may be explained through the interaction between dominant and recessive genes. Once the more recently arriving Asians and others (haplogroups A-D) began interbreeding with the prior, more ancient Native Americans (haplogroup X), the recessive genes of blonde/red hair and blue eyes all but completely disappeared. Despite this dilution of recessive traits, there is still some evidence of this earlier racial type in some Native Americans living today.

With a population of over 300,000 in Chile, the Araucano appear to be one of the most significant remnant populations of this previous age of blonds and red heads in the new world. Elsewhere, native Americans have a lesser degree of this Caucasoid heritage, although many Native North Americans are tall with long narrow skulls, characteristic features of these early Solutrean types. Most native Americans are blood group O (European) and not B (Asian). The Araucano are also up to around 20% Rhesus negative, putting them up there with the Basques as being among the most closely related genetically to the original Upper Paleolithic Europeans.

Not only is Rhesus negative a recessive gene, but blond hair, red hair, green and blue eyes are all recessive genes and any interbreeding with melanin-dominant brown eyed/black haired individuals, will lead to the disappearance of these visual characteristics, but they can still be detected genetically.

Due to isolation of these early inhabitants, they became vulnerable to widespread disease brought in from outside America. This process was also observed in the Pacific by the early explorers. First accounts of Tahiti indicated that over ten percent of the Population was Caucasoid, but when another ship arrived 8 months later, most of these Native Caucasians-types had already succumbed to disease brought by the earlier European ship. Despite this, Polynesians placed these people in high esteem and they were often found in positions of power within Polynesian society.

RHESUS NEGATIVE BLOOD FACTOR

Each person's blood is one of four major types: A, B, AB, or O. Blood types are determined by the types of antigens on the blood cells. Antigens are proteins on the surface of blood cells that can cause a response from the immune system. The Rh factor is a type of protein on the surface of red blood cells. Most people are Rh-positive. Those who do not have the Rh factor are Rh-negative.

The Rh blood group system (including the Rh factor) is one of the currently 30 human blood group systems. The commonly used terms Rh factor, Rh positive and Rh negative refer to the D antigen only. Individuals either have, or do not have, the "Rh factor" on the surface of their red blood cells. Nearly 85% of all human beings have RH positive blood. Their red blood cells contain a substance called the Rhesus blood factor. This means the positive blood contains a protein that was first discovered in the Rhesus monkey, but is not exclusive to it. The antigen is common among all primates. Though chimpanzees, for example, also have different blood groups, they are not the same as human blood types.

Rh-negative has been a subject worthy of attention to pregnant Rh-negative mothers who carry an Rh-positive child. In such cases, there may be a need to administer special shots to prevent the mother's own antibodies from killing the fetus. A mother that is Rh-negative may develop antibodies to an Rh-positive baby and if a small amount of the baby's blood mixes with hers, an immune reaction may respond as if she were allergic to the baby. The mother's body may make antibodies to the Rh antigens in the baby's blood. This means her antibodies can cross the placenta and attack the baby's blood. They break down the fetus's red blood cells and produce anemia, a potentially fatal condition when the blood has a low number of red blood cells.

This condition is called hemolytic disease or hemolytic anemia. It can become severe enough to cause serious illness, brain damage, or even death in the fetus or newborn.(103) This complication has contributed to worldwide speculation of the origin of this unusual blood-type, and rightly so.

Blood factors are transmitted with exactitude, much more so than any other characteristic. If mankind evolved from the same ancestral popula-

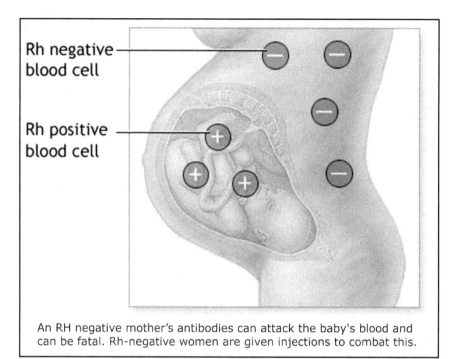

Rh negative blood cell

Rh positive blood cell

An RH negative mother's antibodies can attack the baby's blood and can be fatal. Rh-negative women are given injections to combat this.

FIGURE 34

tion, then one would expect to find that their blood would be more similar, but it's not, which anyone who has ever needed a blood transfusion can attest to. In Blood of the Gods, Mabel Royce asks:

All other earthly primates also have this Rh factor. But this leaves out the people who are Rh negative. If all mankind evolved from the same ancestor their blood would be compatible. Where did the Rh negatives come from? If they are not the descendants of prehistoric man, could they be the descendants of the ancient astronauts? (152)

If the introduction of RH-negative blood type is not a naturally occurring part of terrestrial evolution, which does not seem to be the case, then was it introduced by an outside source? The Cro-magnon people of the Paleolithic ocean-born migration, which populated the northwest coast of

Europe, had this very special blood peculiarity that their descendants are still living with today. This was the only tribe in the world with many, if not all, of its members having Rh-negative blood.(146) Dr. Luigi Cavalli-Sforza published a map of the populations with the frequency percentage of Rh-negative blood.(104) He wrote:

Rh-negative genes are frequent in Europe, infrequent in Africa and West Asia, and virtually absent in East Asia and among the aboriginal populations of Australia. One can estimate degrees of relatedness by subtracting the percentage of Rh-negative individuals among, say, the English (16%) from that among the Basques (25%) to find a difference of 9% points. But between the English and East Asians it becomes 16% points, a greater distance that perhaps implies a more ancient separation.(104)

According to numerous sources, Rh negative blood stems from Upper Paleolithic, or Cro-Magnon man.(100) By looking at Rh negative blood type frequencies in different population demographics, it might become possible to identify a geographic origin. On a national level, Australia tops the percentage of Rh negatives with 19%. Among some of the blond tribes still living in the Atlas Mountains of Morocco called Berbers, that percentage is doubled to 40%. Keep in mind it is not a national average, but restricted to certain local tribes. Another group with legitimate claims of highest rate of Rh negative blood are the Basques of the Pyrenees Mountains, reported in different publications as having up to 32%, depending on location. The people of northwest Ireland, the Highland Scots and the western islanders of Norway all have between 16 and 25%, while the Lapps of Norway and Finland have between around 7%. (145) Comprehensive studies of blood types in the Americas also show that Mayans, Incas, and Auracanians (natives of Chile) have/had 5-20% of the population being Rh negative. (147) Based on data published in, *Distribution of the ABO and rhesus (D) blood groups in the north of Scotland,* by Elizabeth S Brown, the frequency of Rh negatives in Scotland varies between the low number of

10.28% on the Moray Coast to 30.44% Rh negatives in the Inverness region on the west coast.(146) Last, but certainly not least, are many populations of Jewish people, such as the Jewish Karaites of Iraq, which also rank among the densest Rh negative tribes in the world.

Here are 8 regional populations that have a higher than 20% rate of RH negative blood type.

1. The Berbers, namely the Ait Haddidu Berbers in the Atlas mountain region of Morocco, have a percentage of Rh negatives reaching as high as 40%.
2. Basque territory, located in the Pyrenees mountain region of Spain and France, has around 35% Rh negative population in the higher regions.
3. Scotland has more than 20% Rh negatives in Oxnard and the Isle of Mull, but can reach as high as 30% in Iverness.
4. Although close by with many similarities (R1b), Northern Ireland is on a separate island, and its published statistics on its RH negative population is at 27%.
5. In Switzerland, the towns of Tenna, Versam and Safien in the Rhone Valley show a frequency of the Rh negative blood frequency at 26.5%.
6. The Dutch municipality Bunschoten-Spakenburg in the Netherlands has 20,000 inhabitants; 25% are Rh negative.
7. Catalonians, part of an autonomous community of Spain, just make the list topping 20% being Rh negative.
8. A study in the 1950s examining a little bit more than 100 Karaite Jews (R1a Haplogroup) revealed the percentage of Rh negative within that group somewhere around 28%.

We could have descendants of ice age Atlanteans scattered throughout the massive continents of North and South America. All modern scientific theories choose to ignore the possibility of a large Cro-Magnon-populated land mass (Atlantis) lying in the central North Atlantic, which could easily have provided migrations of Cro-Magnon populations in both directions (to Europe and America) during the ice age. (102)

Edgar Cayce, the famous American mystic known as the "Sleeping prophet", had suggested that some of the people that fled the sinking continent went west and settled and became the Iroquois. Others went east to the Iberian Peninsula then the Pyrenees (Basques), and the West Coast of North Africa (Guanches), and the Atlas Mountains (Berbers). (144)

THE BASQUE

Nestled in the mountains between France and Spain, there is a semi-isolated population of native European people that have long puzzled anthropologists, linguists, and historians, because although they are Caucasoid, they do not fit in with the rest of the European populations. Their language, for example, is distinctly unique in Europe and not related to any other Indo-European tongue. But that is not the only thing that is unique about the Basque.

Prior to the advent of genetic research tools, investigators used the ABO blood groups to study the relationships between human populations as well as their migration patterns. The Basques turned out to also be unique in terms of blood. As a population they contain among the highest levels of Rh- negative blood in the world and among the lowest type B. These people currently inhabit the the area surrounding Pyrenees mountains, where Cro magnon left behind some of his/her most famous artwork over 30,000 years ago. But exactly who are the Basque and where did they come from?

I decided that a great place to find out is the University of Nevada, since it houses the Center for Basque Studies. This organization is primarily a research center that conducts and publishes on Basque-related topics such as anthropology, history, cultural studies, etc. Here is what they had to say about the Basque people and their origins; this from their website's FAQ:

Question: Who are the Basques?
Answer: "The Basques are a people who live in a small region (about the size of Rhode Island) that straddles the border of Spain and France from

the sea in the west into the Pyrenees in the east. This area is called Euskal Herria (comprising seven provinces). Basques speak a language called Euskara, but today only about 25% of the population is fluent in that language. The Basque population is distinguished physically by a high incidence of Rh Negative factor in the blood."(108)

Question: Where do the Basque come from?
Answer: "No one knows exactly where the Basques came from. Some say they have lived in that area since Cro-Magnon man first roamed Europe. Some say they are descended from the original Iberians. More fanciful theories exist, as well. One is that the Basques are the descendents of the survivors of Atlantis. "(108)

Question: Where does the Basque language come from?
Answer: "Just as no one is sure about the origins of the Basques themselves, linguists are not in agreement over the origins of Euskara, the Basque language, either. Although there are theories (none of them proven beyond a doubt) that Basque is related to other languages (such as the Georgian family of languages in the Caucasus, or the Berber language family [Cro-Magnon Atlanteans] of Africa, or even the Quechua language of Latin America). "(108)

When asked, I've found that the majority of the Basque people themselves maintain that they came from "Atlaintika", a powerful maritime nation that sank into the Atlantic Ocean after a terrible cataclysm and from which a few survivors reached the Bay of Biscay and the Pyrenees mountains. This, they say, is not just mythology but their true pre-European ancestry. (107)

It may be true that the Basque language, Euskara, is unrelated to any Indo-European speech, however it does seem to share some affinity with Finno-Urgic Patumnili (spoken in ancient Troy), Etruscan (possibly descended from the Trojans), Guanche (spoken by the prior/first native inhabitants of the Canary Islands), Nahuatl, the language of the Aztecs, and amazingly the Ainu native indigenous inhabitants of Japan.(125) These long-dead languages are not well understood today. But the fact that Basque Euskara contains similarities with the languages of at least four presumably Atlantean peoples warrants further investigation. Author Stuart Webb states that:

Atalya It is the name of an ancient ceremonial mound in Biarritz, Basque country. Atalya is also a sacred mountain in the Valley of Mexico venerated by the Aztecs. Atalaia is a site in southern Portugal featuring Bronze Age domed tombs, dating to the thirteenth century BC. Atalya is in Gran Canaria, where pyramids built by the Guanches in black, white, and red volcanic stone (the same construction materials described for Atlantis by Plato) may still by seen. The name Italy derives from Atalia, when, according to Etruscan tradition, Atlas ruled there in prehistory. Italy means, literally, "the Domain of Atlas," whose daugher was Atlantis. (153)

Prof. Henry Fairfield Osborn (1915-1923), declared that the Cro-Magnon people of the Stone Age left two cultural "relics" that survived into modern times: The first being the Berber-speaking Guanches of the Canary Islands, and secondly, the unique Basque language of western Europe. In regard to the extreme age of the Basque language, the distinguished British scholar Michael Harrison once wrote:

In support of the theory that Basque, if not an autochthonous (native) language, is at least one of the most primitive languages of Europe, in the sense of its being here before any of the existing others, is the fact that Basque... is still a language with no proven congeners. (109)

Looking at the linguistic and other cultural connections by such widely diverse and otherwise unrelated peoples as the Basque, Guanches, Aztecs, and Etruscans, one might possibly conclude that all of them were impacted earlier in their histories by culture bearers from Atlantis. Is is now clear that "Atalia" carries the same connotation in Euskara, Nahuatl, Iberian, and Guanche: the description of a sacred mound-like structure, or mountain. Is it not reasonable to suspect that these peoples all fell within the Atleantean sphere of influence? The Euskara's resemblance to certain North American Indian languages, particularly Algonquin-Lenape, is also established.(125) R. Cedric Leonard considers the linguistic connections:

The extinct Iberian language, which are found on ancient clay tablets, is also considered to be related to modern Basque. Is this language a version of one spoken by an earlier stage of Cro-Magnon man? While the meanings and definitions of words are considered to be primitive, the actual syntax is extremely complex and orderly. Both the Romans and Carthaginians recorded that Basque was originally very widespread, including affinities with the Morracan Berbers of North Africa. (125)

Prof. Johannes Friedrich, the leading linguist and expert on Berber, claims the language has not changed in almost 2000 years. Welsh, Erse, and Gaelic use the same complicated syntax that Basque does. The people living in the British Isles used that language long before the Kelts arrived in 1800 BC. Welsh is peculiar in that it adopted Celtic words into its vocabulary, but maintained the syntax. It is suggested by a growing number of linguists that pre-Celtic Welsh was identical to Basque.

The Maya continue to this day to speak their language, and to the surprise of a Basque missionary during the 1500s come to convert them, found that they spoke a very similar language, with a slight difference in pronunciation.

Both the Greeks and the Basques of ancient times shared astrotheological myths, such as the first people were centaurs. The very word centaur is derived from the Basque word Zalzaval (horse-man). Many prehistoric cave paintings in the Pyrenees depict the horse, and one of the oldest Basque festivals (the Rigodon dance) features a man in the horse costume (zamalzain, the horse-man) dancing around a cup, variously referred to as the Grail. In fact, the Basques used to refer to themselves as the descendents of the Centaurs (Cantavres), who came to earth in the center of an ancient island. Plato writes of horse domestication and even horse races in Atlantean times.

American Linguist R. Cedric Leonard has much to say on the subject, coining the term "Berber-Ibero-Basque Language Complex" and attempting to identify the earliest patterns of linguistics linking Europe and the Mediterranean:

The various dialects of what I believe was the original language of the Atlanteans accompanied the Cro-Magnon people as they swept into the western portions of Europe and Africa from Atlantis. The remains of this phenomenon exist to this day in what I call the Berber-Ibero-Basque Language Complex. This complex stretched from Morocco in North Africa, across Gibraltar into the Iberian peninsula, on up into the Dordogne Valley of France and Brittany, continuing northward to the British Isles. If such an Atlantic language did exist, we will have identified the Atlantean language, at least provisionally. At the very least, we can ask if such a unified, widespread language did not come from Atlantis, from where did it come?(115)

Noting that the tribes of Berbers of North Africa were also of Cro Magnon lineage, R. Cedric Leonard goes on to say:

Professional anthropologists have already postulated, in a classic work on European ethnology, that the modern day Basque people of the Pyrenees Mountains (northern Spain/southern France) speak a language inherited directly from Cro-Magnon Man. To give a couple of illustrative examples of the reasons for the above postulation, the Basque (Euskara) word for knife means literally "stone that cuts," and their word for ceiling means "top of the cavern." (106)

〰〰〰〰〰〰〰〰〰〰〰〰〰〰〰〰〰〰〰〰〰〰〰〰〰〰〰〰〰〰〰〰〰〰〰

Ethnologist Michael A. Etcheverry states his opinion that the Basques, having fought off assimilation by the Romans, Visigoths, Moors and Franks, were themselves:

〰〰〰〰〰〰〰〰〰〰〰〰〰〰〰〰〰〰〰〰〰〰〰〰〰〰〰〰〰〰〰〰〰〰〰

The direct descendants of the Ice Age Cro-Magnon people who had, more than any others, avoided both the modification of their genetic makeup and their language during the following era of Neolithic expansion. (104)

〰〰〰〰〰〰〰〰〰〰〰〰〰〰〰〰〰〰〰〰〰〰〰〰〰〰〰〰〰〰〰〰〰〰〰

The famous German philologist Wilhelm von Humboldt was convinced of the existence of a single great Iberian people in ancient times, speaking a distinct non-European language of their own. He proposed that these ancient Iberian people once extended through southern France into Brittany, and on into the British Isles, even including the Mediterranean islands of Sicily, Sardinia and Corsica. Humboldt also contended that the Basques of modern times are remnants of that "once wide-spread Atlantic seaboard population".(110) German Anthropologist Otto Muck adds some more insight into the origins of Basque:

〰〰〰〰〰〰〰〰〰〰〰〰〰〰〰〰〰〰〰〰〰〰〰〰〰〰〰〰〰〰〰〰〰〰〰

According to Finck (one of the greatest authorities on comparative philology), the lesser-known languages of the prehistoric inhabitants of the Mediterranean region are distantly related to ancient Basque, and we know that the oldest Italic aboriginal tribe was called Osci, identical with Ausci and Vascones. (118)

〰〰〰〰〰〰〰〰〰〰〰〰〰〰〰〰〰〰〰〰〰〰〰〰〰〰〰〰〰〰〰〰〰〰〰

If we take these and all the foregoing facts into account, we begin to get a picture of a worldwide complex of linguistic relationships that transcend time and space. We can see Basque, an oddity among modern European languages, as the last relic of a prehistoric world language that was spoken on both sides of the Atlantic."(118) Otto Muck then shares this:

Can we find any solid reasons for believing that here, in the Basques, a relic of Atlantis has been preserved? The Basques themselves provide one: they still have a clear memory of Atlantis. (118)

Ernst von Salomon mentions, this in his travel book Boche in Frankreich (Boche in France). In about the year 1930, he met a Basque smuggler with aquiline features who talked to him about his people. Von Salomon continues:

The Basques, he said, are the last relics of a more beautiful, freer, prouder world, long ago sunk below the sea together with Atlantis, one of whose last remaining pillars was the Pyrenees, and the other the mountain of Morocco.(118)

It should be noted that the Basques and civilizations far away, such as the Aryans of India that had never been in physical contact with each other, living in widely separated areas, yet both have the ancient swastika symbol in common, as well as a plethora of linguistic affinities. Therefore, the characteristics they shared with the distant cultures must have been acquired from a common source which, in my opinion, must have been a global sea-faring civilization; possibly Atlantis. According to the famous linguist Louis Farrar:

The fact is indisputable and is eminently noteworthy, that while the affinities of the Basque roots have never been conclusively elucidated, there has never been any doubt that this isolated language, preserving its identity in a western corner of Europe, between two mighty kingdoms, resembles, in its grammatical structure, the aboriginal languages of the vast opposite continent [America].(117)

In 1940, Alexander Braghine wrote in his book, *The Shadow of Atlantis*, the following about native tribal linguistics:

◇◇◇

When in Guatemala, I often heard about one Indian tribe, living in the Peten district (Northern Guatemala): this tribe speaks a language resembling Basque, and I have heard of an occasion when a Basque missionary preached in Peten in his own idiom with great success.(116)

◇◇◇

Alexander Braghine goes on to compare the language of the Basque to what is spoken by people in Japan and Mexico:

◇◇◇

As to the resemblance of the Japanese and Basque languages, I once saw a list of analogous words with the same significance in both tongues and I was stupefied by the quantity of such words. The word 'iokohama', for instance, signifies in Basque 'seashore city', and everybody knows the great port of Yokohama in Japan. A very interesting Indian tribe called the Otomis lives in the neighborhood of Tula in Mexico: these Indians speak the old Japanese idiom, and once when the Japanese ambassador to Mexico visited this tribe he talked with them in this old dialect. Taking into consideration all these facts and observations, I would like to offer the following conjecture. It is likely that the emigration from Atlantis developed in two directions, eastwards and westwards. (116)

◇◇◇

THE BERBERS

Modern Cro-Magnon people can be found in certain parts of Western Europe, North Africa and some of the Atlantic Islands today. Physical anthropologists agree that Cro-Magnon is represented in modern times by the populations such as the Berber and Tuareg peoples of North Africa, the recently extinct Guanches of the Canary Isles, the Basques of northern Spain, the Aquitanians living in the Dordogne Valley and Brittany in France; and until lately, those living on the Isle d'Oleron. This indicated by obviously Cro-Magnon-like skulls. (125,126)

The Berbers are currently located geographically around Mount Atlas, but inhabited much of North Africa long before the Arabs arrived. The Berbers are considered the aboriginals of the area and their origins beyond that are not officially known. Many theories have been advanced relating them to the Canaanites, the Phoenicians, the Celts, and the Caucasians from Anatolia. In classical times the Berbers formed such states as Mauritania and Numidia. It is unfortunate that the Berbers have not received more attention from science over the years. Here we have a Caucasoid race, many of whom have blue eyes and light hair, living in North West Africa, of all places. Anthropologists for the most part dismissed them for many years because they did not fit well with the 'Out of Africa' paradigm, so it was presumed that they had back migrated from somewhere in Europe. However, that theory has been abandoned with the current understanding of genetics. Scientists now generally accept the genetic evidence that concludes Berbers are an indigenous people, which they believe are descended from native Upper Paleolithic people straight back into the Pleistocene (ice age). (124)

They are an ancient people with a very high frequency of haplogroup X and Rh negative blood type. Among the Berbers, the lightest skin pigmentation recorded is that of the Rifians, the Berbers retaining the most recessive traits (European-looking). Ten percent have light brown or blond hair: the blonds tend to be golden, or reddish.(124) Concerning "blondism" among the Berbers, Dr. Jean Hiernaux, the Director of Research at the National Center for Scientific Research in Paris, writes:

The relatively high incidence of blondism in North Africa has raised much speculation. Has it evolved locally, or does it represent an admixture of European elements from an area where blondism has a high incidence? Both views are tenable.(124)

The Cro Magnon distribution map shows archeological sites in northern Morocco. Those are today the Berbers. Authors have often times been of the opinion that both Iberian and Basque originated in Berber country. Why? Because of the affinities which exist between those two languages and the modern Berber tongue. But even though these languages are apparently related, why imagine they all originated in North Africa? (104) A glance at any map of the Atlantic ocean will show the geographical proximity of these areas to Plato's Atlantis. If Cro-Magnon simultaneously appeared on the western shores of both continents, as most physical anthropologists insist, then so did his language. (104) No evidence has been found to indicate that Cro-Magnon's origin was in North Africa, so why would his language originate there? (102)

THE CANARY ISLAND GUANCHES

The Guanches were very tall, powerfully built, blond and red haired indigenous natives of the Canary Islands: specifically the island of Teneriffe. Early Spanish accounts seem to indicate at least three distinct populations, each inhabiting different islands, and that one group exhibited physical traits also seen in northern European populations.

One of the earliest reports of the Canary islands comes from Pliny who, in the 1st century, spoke of an expedition sent by the King of Mauritania, which brought back giant dogs as a souvenir of the trip. This is the origin of the name of the islands: Canary Islands, from Can or Canes. Magnificent examples of these native domesticated hunting dogs can still be found in the islands, where they are called "verdinos" on some islands and "bardinos" on others.

To date there is still no evidence that the Guanches had boats or any knowledge of maritime technology, which begs the question; how did they get there? This isolation allowed the Guanche to maintain a racial exclusivity until the time of the Spanish conquest, however the name came to be incorrectly applied to the indigenous populations of ALL the islands. The name comes from:

GUAN = Person

CHINET = Teneriffe, or "Man of Teneriffe"

According to the Encyclopedia Britannica (11th edition) concerning the ethnic origins and racial identity of the Canary Island Guanches: "The Guanches are thought to be of Cro-Magnon origin.. with blue or gray eyes, and blondish hair". (32)

Isolated in their islands, the Guanches preserved their pristine Cro-Magnon genetic traits in a more or less pure fashion until the arrival of the Spanish. Just about exterminated by the Spaniards at the turn of the 15th century, these people left behind not only pyramid structures in stone, but also mummies. It is hard to miss the resemblance between the Egyptian, Mayan, and Guanche cultures in their usage of pyramids and mummification of their dead.

Lava stone pyramids on Tenerife, researched by Thor Heyerdahl

FIGURE 36

Found primarily in caves (not in the pyramids), Guanche mummies once numbered in the thousands. Today only a handful remain, mostly in museum collections (which probably won't be on display). The scientific study of Guanche mummies has been almost nonexistent, the following information is based only on the mummies discovered on Tenerife.

There, the Guanches removed the internal organs of their royalty, or members of their highest society. Bodies were embalmed in red ochre and were most likely dried out in the sun first. At the end of the process, the mummy was wrapped in animal skins, such as goat skins; kings received 10-15 skins, other individuals received many fewer. Then it was placed in a cave on a special mummy board. Finally, a stone wall was erected around the mummy. These factors (drying, cave burial, stone wall) also helped insure that the mummy would be preserved. (128)

Today, due to some intermarriage, some traits of the Cro Magnon still appear, such as when individuals will sometimes be taller and blond. But for the most part, the culture of the Guanches was wiped out. What remains can be found on the island's main museum, which according to their own promotional literature, is also home to the "World's Largest Collection of Cro-magnon Skulls." Professor Retzius in an 1859 issue of the Smithsonian Report:

⟨⟩

With regard to the primitive dolichocephal those who have a head unusually long (front to back) relative to width (as does Cro-Magnon)] of America, I entertain a hypothesis still more bold, namely, that they are nearly related to the Guanches of the Canary Islands, and to the Atlantic populations of Africa, the Moors, Tuaricks, Copts, which Latham comprises under the name of Egyptian-Atlantic We find one and the same form of skull in the Canary Islands, in front of the African coast, and in the Carib islands, on the opposite coast which faces Africa. (129)

⟨⟩

Madam Blavatsky, one of the most famous occult researchers of the 19th century, points out the genetic relations between these populations well over 100 years before our modern understanding of DNA:

〰〰〰〰〰〰〰〰〰〰〰〰〰〰〰〰〰〰〰〰〰〰〰〰〰〰〰〰〰

If, then, Basques and Cro-Magnon Cave-Men are of the same race as the Canarese Guanches, it follows that the former are also allied to the aborigines of America. This is the conclusion which the independent investigations of Retzius, Virchow, and de Quatrefages necessitate. The Atlantean affinities of these three types become patent. (130)

〰〰〰〰〰〰〰〰〰〰〰〰〰〰〰〰〰〰〰〰〰〰〰〰〰〰〰〰〰

Madame Helena Petrovna Blavatsky

FIGURE 37

Here, once again, she is quite clear as to where the Guanches originally came from long before the human genome was sequenced and proper
DNA analysis could be carried out:

◇◇

The Guanches were lineal descendants of the Atlanteans. This fact
will account for the great stature evidenced by their old skeletons,
as well as by those of their European congeners the Cro-Magnon
Paleolithic men. (130)

◇◇

And finally, Blavatsky claims that all of European Paleolithic man, or
ice age Europeans, are of Atlantean ancestry:

◇◇

Paleolithic European man of the Miocene and Pliocene times was
a pure Atlantean, as we have previously stated. The Basques are, of
course, of a much later date than this, but their affinities, as here
shown, go far to prove the original extraction of their remote ancestors. (130)

◇◇

Chapter 5

One of the oldest documented prehistoric symbols is perhaps most famously known as the 'Swastika' in India, but also the 'Fylfot' in England, the 'Hakenkreuz' in Germany, the 'Tetra Gammadion' in Greece, the 'Wan' in China, and the 'Manji' in Japan. In his 1896 book called, *The Swastika: The Earliest Known Symbol and its Migrations*, Thomas Wilson, curator of the Department of Prehistoric Anthropology in the U.S. National Museum, wrote:

> An Aryan symbol used by the Aryan peoples before their dispersion through Asia and Europe. This is a fair subject for inquiry and might serve as an explanation how as a sacred symbol the Swastika might have been carried to the different peoples and countries in which we now find it by the splitting up of the Aryan peoples and their migrations and establishment in the various parts of Europe.(194)

This sacred solar symbol has been an object of profound veneration among widely dispersed ancient cultures from the earliest times. It is seen

| India | Russia | Germany | USA | Greece |

| Poland | Navaho | Tibet | Peru | Hittie |

| Thracian | Saxon | Korea | Iran | Italy |

| Aztec | Ethiopia | Japan | Anasazi | Basque |

| Sumer | Hopewell | Israel | Armenia | Apache |

Swastika symbol represented in cultures world wide

FIGURE 38

on Buddhist zodiacs, and is one of the symbols in the Asoka inscriptions. It is the sectarian mark of the Jains, and the distinctive badge of the sect of Xaca Japonieus. The Vaishnaves of India have also the same sacred sign, also adored by the followers of the Lama of Tibet. North of Mexico, it occurs amongst the Mixtecos and in Queredaro. Siguenza mentions an Indian cross which was found in the cave of Mixteca Baja. Among the ruins on the island of Zaputero in Lake Nicaragua were also found similar crosses reverenced by the Indians. The swastika symbol was used by the Aztecs and was on the coat of arms of the Mexican state of Sonora around 1930.

Pre-Columbian Hopewell Green Slate Serpent Swastika
Origin: The Mississipi Valley, USA Circa: 200 BC

FIGURE 39

Swastika shaped artifacts have been found in excavations of sites in the Ohio and Mississippi River valleys. It was also widely used by many southwestern tribes, most notably the Hopi and the Navajo. After learning of the Nazi association, and political leverage from the US government, the Navajo discontinued use of the symbol.(14) In South America the same sign was considered symbolical and sacred. It was revered in Paraguay. Among the Muyscas at Cumana, various crosses were regarded with devotion and believed to be endowed with power to drive away evil spirits; consequently new-born children were placed under the sign.(166)

A swastika composed of Hebrew letters as a mystical symbol from the Jewish Kabbalistic work "Parashat Eliezer." The symbol is enclosed by a circle and surrounded by a cyclic hymn in Aramaic. The hymn, which refers explicitly to the power of the Sun, as well as the shape, shows strong solar symbolism.

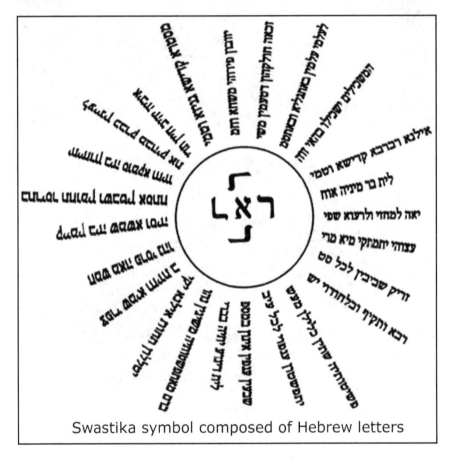

Swastika symbol composed of Hebrew letters

FIGURE 40

This mandala-like symbol is an adaptation from the early Hebrew symbol meaning "eternity in motion", and is meant to help a mystic to contemplate on the cyclic nature and structure of the Universe. The letters are the initial and final characters of the Hebrew word for 'light'.

On the eastern slope of the Andes mountains in northern Peru, forests cloak the ruins of a pre-Inca civilization, the size and scope of which explorers and archaeologists are only now beginning to understand. Known as the Chachapoya, the civilization covered an estimated 25,000 square miles (65,000 square kilometers). They were distinguished by fair skin, great height, and how they lived; in stone circle houses primarily on ridges and mountain tops.(181)

Swastika-adorned pottery on display at a Peruvian museum.

FIGURE 41

97

The name Chachapoya is in fact the name that was given to this culture by the Inca; the name that these people may have used to refer to themselves is not known. They are nicknamed the "Warriors of the Clouds" or the "Cloud People".(182) Pedro Ciezo de Leon (1520 to 1554) was one of the earliest and most prolific of the Spanish chroniclers, and wrote about the Chachapoyas:

They are the whitest and most handsome of all the people that I have seen in the Indies, and their wives were so beautiful that because of their gentleness, many of them deserved to be the Incas' wives and to also be taken to the Sun Temple.(182)

Accounts such as that of Cieza de Leon indicate that the Chachapoyas had lighter skin than other South American peoples, blue or green eyes, and blond hair. This poses an enduring mystery for scholars of the region as to their ultimate origin. The Chachapoyas were killed by epidemics of European diseases, such as measles and smallpox, soon after the Spanish Arrived. Since they had sided with the conquistadors against their enemy the Inca, this close proximity to the Spanish may have proved especially fatal.

Guanche mummy of the Museo Nacional de Antropología (National Museum of Anthropology) in Madrid, Spain

FIGURE 42

Much of their way of life was also destroyed by pillaging, leaving little for archaeologists to examine. However, intact skeletons have been found, some that even show clear evidence of ancient bone surgery. A cache of more than 200 mummies was found in Peru in late 1996 by machete wielding grave robbers cutting through the cloth wrappings, looking for jewelry and other treasures. (183,185)

The mummies were originally discovered in cave-like niches set in a cliff in an area of northern Peru called Laguna de los Cedores near Leymebamba. The people seemed to have purposefully selected dry caves for the burials.(184)

Another group of Chachapoya mummies were discovered in late 2006 by a farmer in a burial cave complex some 82 feet below the earth's surface. The cave is known as Iyacyecuj, or "enchanted water", by local people. When team leader and Archeologist Herman Corbera was interviewed, he remarked: "This is a discovery of transcendental importance. It is the first time any kind of underground burial site this size has been found belonging to Chachapoyas or other cultures in the region."(185)

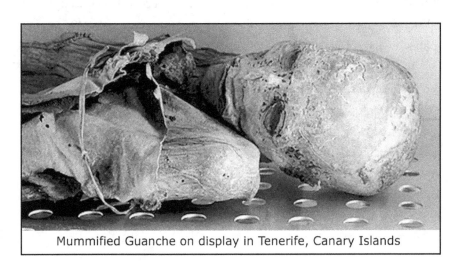

Mummified Guanche on display in Tenerife, Canary Islands

FIGURE 43

Peruvian archaeologist Sonia Guillen had a chance to work on the site with the actual mummies herself and said: "Two of the mummies are more than a thousand years old. Some of the mummies have become skeletons, others were preserved in funerary bundles."(184)

In 2007, an article was published about the most recent find, the "biggest free-standing Chachapoya structure in the world. The structure was nick-named the 'Huaca la Penitenciaria de la Meseta' (The Penitentiary) by its discoverers because of its tall stone walls. It consists of two rectangular cer-emonial platforms on one side of a plaza in the middle of a plateau called La Meseta, not the mountaintops usually associated with the Chachapoya, about 6,000 feet above sea level on the eastern side of the Andes. The site, likely a town or ceremonial center, has been covered for centuries by a forest. Since the site is still mostly unexplored, it remains to be seen whether any mummies are inside, though they may well have been prepared here. (185)

There isn't much left of the city of Tiahuanaco in Bolivia. In the 1500's, the Spanish systematically destroyed the buildings. Later, many of the stone blocks were looted for houses in a nearby village. Most recently, more stone was taken to lay a new railroad. Despite this, what is left is still a sight to see. Tiahuanaco is old. It was already in ruins when the Incas took over the area in 1200 A.D.. It is situated on a mountain at an altitude of 12,500 feet and boasts a pyramid 700 feet long, 500 feet wide and 50 feet tall. There is also a temple 440 feet long topped with columns up to 14 feet high that may have once supported a roof.

To me, the most impressive thing about Tiahuanaco isn't its archi-tecture, but the legends surrounding the identity of the builders. Passed down through oral tradition, the stories tell of how the city was originally constructed by a race of tall fair-skinned god-men with beards. He was called Viracocha by the Incas, Kukulkan by the Mayas, Quetzalcoatl by the Aztecs, Gucumatz in Central America, Votan in Palenque and Zamna in Izamal. He, and in some cases his men, were described as being tall, beard-ed, with white skin, and beautiful emerald blue eyes. According to an early European explorer, it was said that Viracocha:

Gave rules to men how they should live, and he spoke lovingly to them with much kindness, admonishing them they should be kind to each other.(187)

100

There are similar stories about visits by a bearded white man among the Aztec and Mayans. He was called Quetzalcoatl by the Aztecs and Kukulcan by the Mayans. Fray Juan Torquemada, the Franciscan missioner, who collected numerous traditions about Quetzalcoatl from the natives of Old Mexico, says: "Quetzalcoatl had blond hair, and wore a black robe sewn with little crosses of red color." How did blond-haired men arrive in Peru long before the Spanish did?

Credo Mutwa, the 94-year-old Zulu shaman or "Sanusi" in South Africa, claims that this picture he had painted of tall, blond-haired, blue-eyed beings had been seen by black African tribes people throughout that continent long before the white Europeans arrived. Credo, an official historian of the Zulu nation, said that when the Europeans first came, the black Africans thought they were the return of these same white "gods", which they called the Mzungu. As a result they called the European settlers by the same name. This was very much the same reaction as the Central Amer-

Image of blond Quetzalcoatl from a public school textbook in Mexico

FIGURE 44

ican peoples when Cortes and his Spanish invasion party arrived in 1519 and they thought that he was the returning god, Quetzalcoatl, who was also described as tall, bearded, and blue eyed.

The Spanish conquistador Francisco Pizarro asked the natives of Peru who the white skinned redheads were. The Inca Indians replied that they were the last descendants of the Viracochas. The Viracochas, they said, were a divine race of white bearded men. They were so like the Spanish that the Europeans were called Viracochas the moment they came to the Inca Empire. The Incas thought they were the Viracochas who had come sailing back across the Pacific. (186)

According to the principal Inca legend, before the reign of the first Inca, the sun-god, Con-Ticci Viracocha, had taken leave of his kingdom in present day Peru and sailed off into the Pacific with all his subjects. The white men had abandoned their pyramids and statues and gone with the leader, Con-Ticci Viracocha, first up to Cuzco, and then down to the Pacific. They were given the Inca name of Viracocha, or "sea foam", because they were white skinned and vanished like foam over the sea. Cuzco is the historic capital city of the Incan empire. Built out of stone and once adorned with gold, it is in southeastern Peru, near the Urubamba Valley of the Andes mountain range. It is a tourist destination and receives one million visitors a year. (186)

Two thousand years ago a mysterious and little known civilization, with a blue-eyed elite, ruled the northern coast of Peru. Its people were called the Moche. They built huge pyramids that still dominate the surrounding countryside; some well over a hundred feet tall. Archeologists working at Peru's Huaca Pucllana ruins recently pulled a blue-eyed mummy from an ancient tomb thought to be from the ancient Wari culture that flourished before the Incas. Piercing blue eyes undimmed by the passing of 1,300 years, this is the "Lady of the Mask" a mummy with striking blue eyes, whose discovery could reveal the secrets of a lost culture at the Huaca Pucllana Pyramid located in Lima, Peru. It is the first time a tomb from the region's Wari culture has been discovered intact and gives historians the chance to learn about the ancient pre-Incan civilizations.

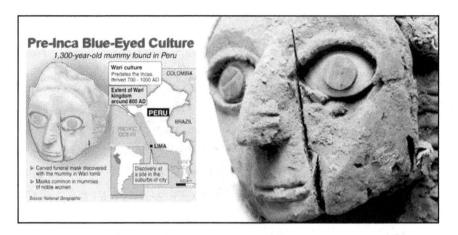

FIGURE 56

One of the first things people notice when exploring the ancient ruins in Peru are the beautiful ashlar blocks for which the Incas are so well known are often sitting directly on top of much larger stones known as polygonal style, which are massive megalithic constructions. The work which

Massive stone walls, Sacsayhuaman, Cusco, Peru

FIGURE 45

is attributed to the Inca culture are primarily 2 ton stone blocks, where the earlier blocks are around 300 tons.(187) Archeologists tend to agree that the larger, earlier, polygonal stone constructions predate the Inca and belong to an earlier culture. Since these earlier constructions have never been dated, no one knows how long they had been there before the Incas.

The size, though impressive, is not the main attraction. The irregular shape and angle of the stones is what usually catches people's eye right away. Some of the blocks have many angles, or sides, and fit together perfectly without the use of any mortar. How was this achieved? What do the locals themselves say?

Thor Heyerdahl was a world famous Norwegian adventurer and ethnographer with a background in zoology, botany, and geography. He became notable for his Kon-Tiki expedition in 1947, in which he sailed 5,000 miles (8,000 km) across the Pacific Ocean in a hand-built raft from South America to the Tuamotu Islands. The expedition shattered long held isolationist theories by demonstrating that ancient people could have made long sea voyages, creating contacts between separate cultures. (186)

Thor's successful, and much celebrated, ocean expedition was linked to a diffusionist model of cultural development, which is supported by modern linguistic, archeological and genetic evidence, but often downplayed in academia. Heyerdahl subsequently made other voyages designed to demonstrate the possibility of contact between widely separated ancient people. In his 1948 classic, *The Kon-Tiki Expedition: By Raft Across the South Seas*, Thor describes the ancient legends concerning the original inhabitants, or gods, of South America.(186)

The Incas acknowledged that the extensive ruins predated their own rise to power. How were these ancients were able to bring such gigantic blocks of stone to the top of the mountain from the quarries many miles away? How were they then able to shape the stones to fit so well together? Hiram Bingham is credited with rediscovering Machu Picchu in 1911, and he relates:

The modern Peruvians are very fond of speculating as to the method which the pre-Incas employed to make their stones fit so perfectly. One of the favorite stories is that the Incas knew of a plant whose juices rendered the surface of a block so soft that the marvelous fitting was accomplished by rubbing the stones together for a few moments with this magical plant juice!(154)

◇◇

Aukanaw, an Argentine anthropologist of Mapuche origin, who died in 1994, related that in Peru, above 4500 m, there is said to be a plant called kechuca which turns stone to jelly, and which the jakkacllopito bird uses to make its nest. A plant with similar properties that grows at even higher altitudes is known, among other things, as punco-punco; this may be Ephedra andina, which the Mapuche consider a medicinal plant.(158)

Researcher Maurice Cotterell, too, believes that pre-Inca and Inca stonemasons possessed the alchemical technology to soften and pour stone. We can do this today but only in one direction, from soft to hard; we call it concrete. It seems that the Incas and the Tiahuanacos could take the process one step further, from hard to soft again, using igneous rocks. (188)

At first this seems incomprehensible, but given the molecular structure of matter it is simply a question of overcoming the covalent bonds that bind atoms together. We can do this to ice, when we turn it to water, and we do it again when we turn water into steam. This may explain how the pre-Incas and Tiahuanacos assembled massive stones with imperfect shapes, with such perfect precision. Close examination of the rounded edges of the stones suggests that the stone material has been poured as though it were once contained within a sack or bag which had long since rotted and disappeared.(159)

Among the ancient cultures of Egypt and South/Central America there were many rituals and practices that were alike, such as circumcision, astrology, and having annual agricultural fairs. A more significant similarity that is common to both cultural areas is the astronomical and directional orientation of edifices. (160)

In Maya culture, knowledge of the heavens developed long before A.D. 250. This knowledge was used in the planning and construction of complex pyramid structures(162). In the pre-Mayan Teotihuacan culture of

Mexico, buildings are grouped along a north-south axis, and in Egypt the Great Pyramids at Cheops are just four minutes west of perfect northerly alignment and have other directional and mathematical relationships to the moon, the planets, and the stars (163).

Burial in underground tombs is a practice common to Egypt, Peru, and Mexico. The rituals of burial in these cultures were also much the same. All three embalmed and mummified their dead. They also went to great extremes to seal tombs so that what was within would be preserved (193).

Many technological developments existed in cultures on both sides of the Atlantic. One example is the using of gold fillings in teeth, which was done in both Egypt and Peru.

The greatest and most obvious technology similarity, however, was the construction of pyramids. Among the pyramids can be found striking similarities. On both sides of the Atlantic ocean, there are step pyramids constructed of several mastaba-like structures. In both cultures many of these step pyramids stand around 200 feet tall, and evidence indicates that they underwent several changes of plan throughout their construction (163).

Pyramid of Kukulcan, Mexico.

FIGURE 46

The use of stones for building the pyramids is also common in both cultures. The stones themselves and the construction techniques used, not only in pyramids but other structures as well exhibit very similar technology. The Egyptians and the Tiahuanaco culture of Peru were capable of building with stones weighing many tons. The precise placement of these stones is equally impressive. The Tiahuanacans fit their stones so precisely that a razor blade could not be slipped between them. In Egypt the stones are so accurately joined that there is never more than 1/50 of an inch between blocks (163).

When noting the relationships between Egypt, South/Central America and Atlantis, it can be found that the legends of Egypt and South/Central America make reference to the origin of the culture. Peruvian legend says that civilizations originators came from the sea. The Egyptians indicate that their ancestors came from the Island of Mero(8). Ignatius Donnelly, who lists 626 references in his book, *Atlantis: The Antediluvian World*, comparing the cultural similarities on both sides of the Atlantic states that: "Both the ancient Egyptian and American Indian cultures originated in Atlantis, and spread east and west when Atlantis was destroyed."

Other legends refer to a geographical connection with this island; they say that there were long bridges of land which joined Africa and South/Central America to Atlantis. Today, there is some evidence that supports the legends of a land bridges. In the area of the Azores islands, 900 miles off the coast of Portugal, between the Gulf of Mexico and the Mediterranean Sea, deep-sea soundings indicate that a great ridge runs south of the Azores for a distance and then divides, sending one arm to South America and the other to Africa (8). A deep-sea core was taken from one place on the ridge and revealed exclusively freshwater diatoms, indicating that part of the ridge was once above sea level.(164)

In 1898, also near the Azores, a ship discovered particles of lava from the sea floor, two miles deep, which had solidified with a vitreous structure. Only when lava solidifies in open air does it assume a vitreous structure. (164) This is eerily similar to what Edge Cayce said in 'readings' that the continent itself extended from South America to Africa.

According to the ancient Egyptian temple records, that come down to us via the writings of Plato, the ancient Athenians fought an aggressive war against the rulers of Atlantis some nine thousand years earlier and won. These ancient and powerful kings or rulers of Atlantis had formed a confederation by which they controlled Atlantis and other islands and colonies as well. They began a war from their homeland in the Atlantic Ocean and sent fighting troops to Europe and Asia.

Against this attack the men of Athens formed a coalition all over Greece to halt it. When this coalition met difficulties, their allies deserted them and the Athenians stood and fought alone to defeat the Atlantean rulers. They stopped an invasion of their own country, as well as freeing Egypt and eventually every other country under the control of the rulers of Atlantis.

New genetic, archeological, and linguistic research has demonstrated that the supposedly discredited diffusion theory may have been scientifically correct after all, even if not politically correct. This theory argues that fair-haired, light-eyed agriculturalists, having tamed the horse and invent-

Similarities in Vocabulary Indicating Close Relationships between Select Indo-European (Aryan) Languages

English	German	Spanish	Greek	Latin	Sanskrit
father	vater	padre	pater	pater	pitar
one	ein	uno	hen	unus	ekam
fire	feuer	fuego	pyr	ignis	agnis
field	feld	campo	agros	ager	ajras
sun	sonne	sol	helios	sol	surya
king	könig	rey	basileus	rex	raja
god	gott	dios	theos	deus	devas

USA	Germany	Spain	Greece	Italy	India

FIGURE 47

ed the wheel, conquered most of Europe, much of the Middle East and Northern India thousands of years ago at the dawn of civilization during the Holocene, bringing with them the family of languages known as Aryan, and are also known as Indo-European/Iranian, spoken from Ireland to India. The Aryan family of languages includes Modern English, German, French, Italian, Irish, Greek, Russian and indeed all European languages apart from Finnish, Hungarian and Basque, together with Iranian, Pashtu, Hindu, Gujarati, Bengali. Sinhalese and other Northern (or originally Northern) Indian languages. The kinship can still be seen in basic words like one, two, three - amhain, dha, tri in Irish, une, deux, trois in French, unus, duo, tres in Latin, eins, zwei, drei in German, einn, tver, thrir in Icelandic, odin, dva, tri in Russian, ena, duo, tria in Greek.

In the ancestor of the Indian branch of this language family, Sanskrit, it's eka, dva, treya. The people who spoke that language swept into the plains of Northern India around 4,000 years ago as chariot-riding conquerors, calling themselves Aryas. On the way they gave their name to Iran, derived from the root "Arya" or Aryan, the Indo-European branch of peoples who settled in that land.

Iran was the ancient name of Persia, and the religion of pre-Islamic Iran was called Zoroastrianism. The name of their prophet was Zarathushtra, the 'stargazer'. The Kings of ancient Iran were very proud to call themselves Aryans, their rock edicts indeed say so, including the famous Behistun Inscription by the Persian king Darius I the Great (522-486) to proclaim his military victories:

I am an Aryan, the son of an Aryan. (174)

The word Aryan occurs time and again in the ancient Iranian scriptures - such as the Yashts (prayers to the divine elements) and the Vendidad (the law against evil). However, all the ancient Zoroastrian scriptures speak of an earlier homeland, the lost "Airyane Vaejahi" or seedland of the Aryans. From this homeland, the Indo-Europeans or Aryans moved to upper

India, Russia and the nations of Europe such as Greece, Italy, Germany, France, Scandinavia, England, Scotland and Ireland.

Bal Gangadhar Tilak was the first popular leader of the Indian Independence Movement. In 1903, he wrote the book The Arctic Home in the Vedas. In it, he argued that the Vedas could only have been composed in the Arctics, and the Aryans brought them south after the onset of the ice age.(239)

Sanskrit, Latin, Avestan are all sister languages, and the present day upper Indian, Persian and European languages are related eg. Baradar in Persian = Brata in Sanskrit = Brother in English. "Persia" is actually a late European term for the language of "Farsi". The Arabic phase in Iran only began 1300 years ago.

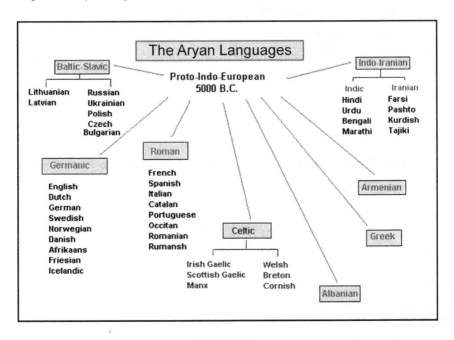

FIGURE 61

The cities of Mohenjo-Daro and Harappa were built by the Aryans who migrated to India, bringing the Vedas with them.(239) They flourished for thousands of years, before succumbing to some other catastrophe(100), or degradation of civilization.

Chapter 6

The presence of Caucasoid haplogroups, both in ancient and recent DNA testing in south Siberia, Siberia, Mongolia, China and south Asia is attested by the recent genetic studies and Mummies from the Altai and the Xinjiang regions only seem to corroborate this fact. Others swept eastward, where for a thousand years an Aryan language, Tocharian, was spoken in what is now Chinese Turkestan. This ancient race of conquerors were blonde-haired, blue-eyed and averaged well over 6 feet tall, as their ancient and perfectly preserved mummified remains clearly indicate. (169)

Some linguists have managed to link the Proto-Indo-Europeans, to the Bronze Age Andronovonovo Culture, based in western Siberia and what is now Kazakhstan. The remains of the people themselves were buried in great mounds, like later Viking and Anglo-Saxon barrows and howes, known as kurgans. These are similar to the ancient native American mounds found scattered all over the Mississippi valley.

Now geneticists have examined the DNA of these Proto-Indo-Europeans extracted from their ancient tombs. The results are revealed in three seminal papers.(170,171,172) It turns out that genetically the Proto-Indo-Europeans buried in the steppe kurgan graves 5,000 years ago were identical with modern Western and Northern Europeans belonging to the Nordic sub-race. The majority had light hair and blue and green eyes. It wasn't until much later that the gene complexes associated with other racial types appeared in the Central Asian steppe north of the deserts and irrigated farming zone.

The mummified remains of the Tocharian speakers in what is now Chinese Turkestan, have blonde and red hair. So, incidentally, did many early Pharaohs of Egypt. It is also clear from the appearance of most speakers of Indo-Aryan languages today in Pakistan, Northern India, Blackburn, and Leicester that significant interbreeding has occurred between conquerors and conquered in the 4,000 years since.

Studies carried out by scientists from the Institute of Forensic Genetics at the University of Copenhagen have concluded that all blue-eyed people share a common ancestor, someone who lived 6,000 to 10,000 years ago near the area near Anatolia. Researchers analyzed and compared the unique genetic make-up of the chromosomes in the iris from 155 blue-eyed individuals from diverse regions such as Denmark, Turkey and Jordan. All of the subjects that participated in the study had the exact same genetic "mutations" in specific chromosomes of the eye with very little variation on the genes, indicating that the "mutation" responsible for blue-eyes first arose and spread relatively recently. Scientists conclude that this blue-eyed family spread out from an area north of the Black Sea following the last ice age.(19) Professor Hans Eiberg of the Department of Cellular and Molecular Medicine at University of Copenhagen explains:

These people were among the proto-Indo-European Aryans who subsequently spread agriculture into western Europe and later rode horses into Iran and India

Blue eyes are a recessive trait, and the gene must be inherited from both parents. (Green eyes involve a related but different gene that is recessive to brown but dominant to blue.) Following the ending of the last Ice Age, many Europeans inherited this rare gene associated with blue-eyed people that differentiated them from the rest of the humanity. That includes many people who express shades of brown, they still carry the gene. Indeed, it appears that the elite and nobility that organized the earliest known agricultural civilizations all shared this trait, seemingly coming from the same bloodline.

When we look to ancient Egypt, arguably one of the world's oldest known civilizations, we find many blond and red-haired mummies. Since WW2, western academia, backed and lobbied by politically motivated forces at the United Nations, has pushed for a politically motivated multicultural egalitarian view of history, which has ignored archeological evidence in favor of political correctness. Even if well intentioned, this false perspective has cast much confusion over human origins: Who we are and how we came to be.

Scientists at Zurich-based DNA genealogy center, iGENEA, have published that King Tut belonged to a genetic profile group known as haplogroup R1b1a2. More than 50 per cent of all men in Western Europe belong to this genetic group as do up to 70 per cent of British men. But among modern-day Egyptians, less than 1 per cent of residents belong to this haplogroup, according to scientists.

King Tut and most Europeans share a common ancestor genetically who lived in the Caucasus region, the blue-eyed race spreading out with

King Tut depicted slaying Nubians, a row of hieroglyphs proclaim:
"The perfect god, the image of the Sun rising over foreign lands, like Re when he appears, crushing the vile land of Kush, shooting his arrows against his enemies."

FIGURE 62

agricultural after the end of the ice age. The geneticists were not sure how Tutankhamun's paternal lineage came to Egypt from its region of origin, though it is clear that technology such as chariots and domesticated horses was introduced from a foreign source.

Another one of the oldest documented civilizations, credited with having the first writing, schools, courts, and many other 'firsts' were the ancient Sumerians of Mesopotamia. The ancient Sumerians thought that blue eyes were a sign of the gods. The Sumerian nobility were blue eyed and fair haired, as most of their busts show. These blue eyed statues are of Sumerians from the early 3rd millennium BC. In 1927, Arthur Keith as quoted in *Ur Excavations:*

They (the Sumerians) certainly belong to the same racial division of mankind as the nations of Europe, they are scions of the Caucasian stock. (173)

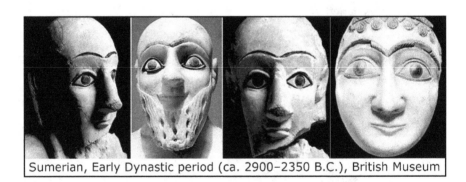

Sumerian, Early Dynastic period (ca. 2900–2350 B.C.), British Museum

FIGURE 50

Gautama Buddha's physical body is traditionally regarded as having the "Thirty-two Characteristics of a Great Man". These 32 characteristics are described throughout the Pali Canon, and are also regarded as being present in Cakravartin kings as well. #29 on this ancient list is "Eyes deep blue."(176)

Bodhidharma was a Buddhist monk who lived during the 5th/6th century. He is credited as the transmitter of Zen Buddhism to China and regarded as its first Chinese patriarch. According to Chinese legend, he also began the physical training of the Shaolin monks that led to the creation of Shaolinquan.

The Anthology of the Patriarchal Hall, considered among the oldest and most authentic Buddhist text, identifies Bodhidharma as the 28th Patriarch of Buddhism in an uninterrupted line that extends all the way back to the Buddha himself. Throughout Buddhist art, he is depicted as profusely bearded with wide-eyes and is referred as "The Blue-Eyed Barbarian" in Chinese Chan texts.(175) New archeological finds in China are forcing a re-examination of old Chinese books that describe historical or legendary figures of great height, with deep-set blue or green eyes, long noses, full beards, and red or blond hair. Scholars have traditionally scoffed at these accounts, but it now transpires that these accounts were correct.(180)

Many people are unaware of the fact that China has massive pyramids that rival Egypt in size and age. The pyramids of China include approximately 100 ancient mounds, many of which are located within 100 kilometers of the city of Xian, on the Qin Chuan Plains in the Shaanxi Province, central China. The pyramids can now be visited on trips from Xian and no longer are located in Forbidden zones Several pyramids have small museums attached to them.

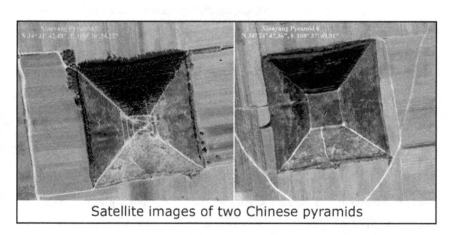

Satellite images of two Chinese pyramids

FIGURE 51

It was in these remote regions that James Churchward (1851-1936) felt he had found evidence of a lost civilization called Mu. For Churchward,

Mu was a lost civilization and continent in the East, which he claimed was 50,000 years old and was the home of 64 million inhabitants. He claimed to have found evidence of this civilization while speaking to a number of Indian men. Though Mu stretched from Micronesia in the West to Easter Island and Hawaii in the East in the Pacific Ocean, knowledge if not descendents of Mankind's original homeland was also meant to be found in India and surrounding regions. He believed that the primary colony of Mu was the Great Uighur Empire and that Khara Khoto was its ancient capital and that the civilization was at its height about 15,000 BC.(25)

Churchward's Mu was not too different from Madam Blavatsky's Lemuria and it was the American Theosophist Gottfried de Purucker (1874 - 1942) who claimed that this region, this enormous tract of country, most of it desert waste, "was once fertile and lush with cities." (180)

The Taklamakan Desert is a large sandy desert, part of the Tarim Basin, a region roughly between Tibet and Mongolia, in Western China, and crossed at its northern and southern edge by the Silk Road. Conditions are so harsh that travelers avoided the desert as much as possible, but in millenia gone by, the region was populated and habitable.

China's landscape is not only littered with enormous pyramids, but hundreds of ancient blond mummies with Caucasoid features. The discoveries in the late 1980s of the undisturbed 4,000-year-old beauty of Loulan and the younger 3,000-year-old body of the Charchan Man are legendary in world archaeological circles for the fine state of their preservation and for the wealth of knowledge they bring to modern research. Many Archaeologists now think they were the citizens of an ancient civilization of Aryans that existed in the east.

Most mummies averaged above 6 feet tall, some were around 6'6" tall. They had long noses and skulls, blond or red hair, thin lips, deep-set eyes, and other unmistakably Caucasian features, like a ginger beard. Dr. Victor H. Mair of the University of Pennsylvania said, "The Tarim Basin Caucasoid corpses are almost certainly representatives of the Indo-European family". Ancient Greek and Chinese historians had long referenced a unique cultural and ethnic group on its western frontier with red hair and blue eyes, a group that settled ancient Afghanistan and forged a vibrant

4,000-year-old Aryan mummy called Beauty of Loulan

FIGURE 52

Buddhist empire that spread Buddhism to much of the the world through China and India. But when 4,000-year-old mummies were unearthed in the early 20th century in the Tarim Basin of the western Chinese desert with Caucasoid physiognomy and clothing of apparently Aryan or Celtic origin, historians, anthropologists, and archeologists were awestruck. The tenuous ethnocultural issue made this a serious matter.

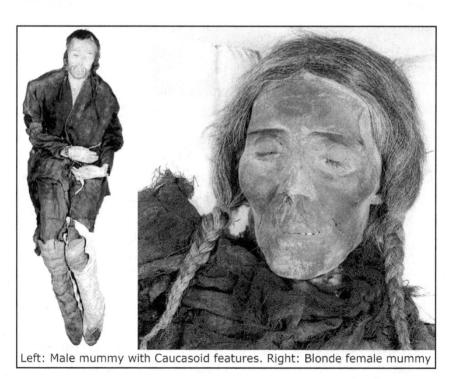

Left: Male mummy with Caucasoid features. Right: Blonde female mummy

FIGURE 53

Modern Chinese scholars refuse to believe that significant foundations of their history were imported, and the modern residents of the Tarim region (Xinjiang), the Uyghurs, insist that they were the original natives of the region. Now it seems that the original inhabitants were both native, as well genetically similar to Europeans (blond, tall, etc), even if they did not invade the territory via Europe during the recent Holocene, having resided there since the Pleistocene (ice age).

We know that they were horsemen and herders, using chariots and may have invented the stirrup. We know that they had dwelled in this region by 1800 BC. That around 1200 BC, the Indo-Europeans were joined by another wave of immigrants, from what is now Iran (the so-called Saka branch). In fact, the Saka nomads had high-pointed hats like the ones found next to Cherchen Man as displayed on the Persepolis reliefs in southern Iran. A bronze statue found in the Altai Mountains from the 5th century BC wore a similar hat. Most important is the fact that the statue had Caucasoid features, and showed similarities in dress to Cherchen Man. The discovery of these mummies indeed rewrote history whether some like the political implications or not.(25) Some appeared to have had blue eyes as shown on Chinese artwork based on the legends of the ancient "gods" that introduced the earliest forms of alchemy, and what later became known as pre-Buddhist philosophy, to the region. The Tocharians are identified as the descendents of these ancient missionaries.

Some major physical evidence we have to determine whether these Buddhist missionaries were related to the mummies is from Chinese frescoes, imagery, and literature depicting what Chinese sources call the Yuezhi and what Greeks called Tocharians as quite foreign in their dress, culture, and appearance. Chinese art shows pale-skinned, red-headed, blue-eyed monks with beards obviously from a race and culture very different from the modern-day Chinese. Sporting partially-shaved heads, dangling earlobes, and the lotus-shaped hand posture, these white Caucasoids are obviously Buddhist monks bringing the new faith to the people along commercial and migratory routes that they had followed when they left the Tarim Basin for Afghanistan.

The mummies in the Small River Cemetery are, so far, the oldest discovered in the Tarim Basin. Carbon tests done at Beijing University show that the oldest part dates to around 4,000 years ago. A team of Chinese geneticists have analyzed the mummies DNA. The maternal lineages were predominantly East Eurasian haplogroup C with smaller numbers of H and K, while the paternal lines were all West Eurasian R1a1a. (192)

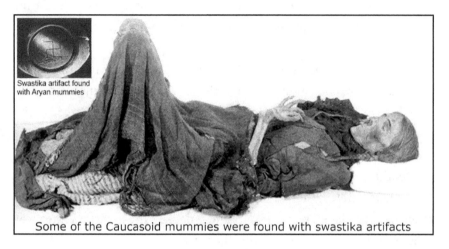

Swastika artifact found with Aryan mummies

Some of the Caucasoid mummies were found with swastika artifacts

FIGURE 54

Professor Victor Mair at the University of Pennsylvania claims that "the earliest mummies in the Tarim Basin were exclusively Caucasoid, or Europoid" with east Asian migrants arriving in the eastern portions of the Tarim Basin around 3,500 years ago while the Uyghur peoples arrived around the year 842. Professor Mair explains claimed that:

The new finds are also forcing a reexamination of old Chinese books that describe historical or legendary figures of great height, with deep-set blue or green eyes, long noses, full beards, and red or blond hair. Scholars have traditionally scoffed at these accounts, but it now seems that they may be accurate.(190)

The Silk Road was an ancient caravan route that connected China to the West. The Caucasoid mummies in this part of the world might suggest

SPECIES WITH AMNESIA: OUR FORGOTTEN HISTORY

that this trade route is indeed older than previously thought very much like trans-oceanic contact was taking place many millenia older than Columbus first voyage to America. According to Dr. Han Kangxin, an anthropologist at the Institute of Archeology in Beijing, the skeletal and mummified evidence clearly points to the fact that the earliest inhabitants of the Tarim Basin region were people are: "Related to the Cro-Magnons of Paleolithic Europe."(177)

This theory is supported by Dr. Victor Mair, a specialist in ancient Asian languages and cultures at the University of Pennsylvania, who stimulated the major search which found the mummies. He has emerged as the main advocate of the theory that large groups of Europeans were present in the Tarim Basin long before the area's present inhabitants.(190)

As the Chinese archaeologists dug through the five layers of burials, Dr. Mair recounted, they came across almost 200 poles, each 13 feet tall. Many had flat blades, painted black and red, like the oars from some great galley that had foundered beneath the waves of sand. At the foot of each pole there were indeed boats, laid upside down and covered with cowhide. The bodies inside the boats were still wearing the clothes they had been buried in. They had felt caps with feathers tucked in the brim. They wore large woolen capes with tassels and leather boots. (190) Within each boat coffin were grave goods, including beautifully woven grass baskets, skillfully carved masks and bundles of ephedra, an herb that may have been used in rituals or as a medicine, as well as several pounds of hemp (marijuana) and poppy (opium). (192)

The language spoken by the people of the Small River Cemetery is unknown, but Dr. Mair believes it could have been Tokharian, an ancient member of the Indo-European (Aryan) family of languages. Manuscripts written in Tokharian have been discovered in the Tarim Basin. The Small River Cemetery people lived more than 2,000 years before the earliest evidence for Tokharian, but there is clear continuity of culture, Dr. Mair said, in the form of people being buried with felt hats, a tradition that continued until the first few centuries A.D.(37)

In her magnum opus, *The Secret Doctrine*, Madam Blavatsky points out in amazing clarity, over a century ago in 1888:

Yet the traces of an immense civilization, even in Central Asia, are still to be found. This civilization is undeniably prehistoric. And how can there be civilization without a literature, in some form, without annals or chronicles? Common sense alone ought to supplement the broken links in the history of departed nations. The gigantic, unbroken wall of the mountains that hem in the whole table-land of Tibet witnessed a civilization during many millennia, and would have strange secrets to tell mankind. The Eastern and Central portions of those regions - the Nan-Schayn and the Altyne-taga [today known as Altyn-tagh] - were once upon a time covered with cities that could well vie with Babylon. A whole geological period has swept over the land, since those cities breathed their last, as the mounds of shifting sand, and the sterile and now dead soil of the immense central plains of the basin of Tarim testify. The borderlands alone are superficially known to the traveler. Within those table-lands of sand there is water, and fresh oases are found blooming there, wherein no European foot has ever yet ventured, or trodden the now treacherous soil. Among these verdant oases there are some which are entirely inaccessible even to the native profane traveler. Hurricanes may "tear up the sands and sweep whole plains away," they are powerless to destroy that which is beyond their reach. Built deep in the bowels of the earth, the subterranean stores are secure; and as their entrances are concealed in such oases, there is little fear that anyone should discover them.

The oasis of Tchertchen, for instance, situated about 4,000 feet above the level of the river Tchertchen D'arya, is surrounded with the ruins of archaic towns and cities in every direction. There, some 3,000 human beings represent the relics of about a hundred extinct nations and races - the very names of which are now unknown to our ethnologists.. the respective descendants of all these antediluvian races and tribes known as little of their own forefathers themselves, as if they had fallen from the moon. When questioned about their origin, they reply that they know not whence their fathers had come, but had heard that their first (or earliest) men were ruled by the great genii of these deserts.

The emplacement of the two cities is now covered, owing to shifting sands and the desert wind, with strange and heterogeneous relics; with broken china and kitchen utensils and human bones. The natives often find copper and gold coins, melted silver, ingots, diamonds, and turquoises, and what is the most remarkable-broken glass.. coffins of some undecaying wood, or material, also, within which beautifully preserved embalmed bodies are found.. the male mummies are all extremely tall powerfully built men with long waving hair. (179)

The Tarim Mummies have destroyed the idea that the West and the East developed independently and that they only relatively recently made contact.(178) The question, however, is whether Europeans went east or a Caucasoid (Cro Magnon) group of people, perhaps native to the Tarim Basin, went to Europe. It may be both, since it is more than likely that we are talking about a globally linked civilization and diffusion.

The Mongol leader Temujin (AD 1167-1227), better known by his title Genghis Khan (Universal Ruler), was, according to the Persian historian Ab ul Ghasi, the tribal clan to which Temujin belonged, were known as the Bourchikoun (Grey-Eyed Men).

GENGHIS KHAN
CONQUEROR

FIGURE 55

The ancestral mother and founder of this clan was known as Alan goa (beautiful Alan). According to the Mongol and Chinese legends on the subject, she was said to have been visited in her tent by a divine being, who possessed golden hair, a fair complexion and gray eyes. Shortly after this visitation, she gave birth to the first member of the Bourchikoun clan.

Temujin himself was noted in Chinese descriptions of him, for his tall stature and heavy beard. We should also note the following depiction of Temujin's appearance, as given by Harold Lamb, in his biography of the great Khan:

He must have been tall, with high shoulders, his skin a whitish tan. His eyes, set far apart under a sloping forehead, did not slant. And his eyes were green, or blue-gray in the iris, with black pupils. Long reddish-brown hair fell in braids to his back.

Ab ul Ghasi also observed that the family of Yesugai, the father of Temujin, were known for the fact that their children often had fair complexions, and blue or gray eyes. Temujin's wife, Bourtai, bore a name which means "Grey-Eyed". Temujin's relatives and descendants also possessed fair features: Temujin's son and successor Ogadei, had gray eyes and red hair; Temujin's grandson Mangu, had reddish eyebrows and a red-brown beard; Subatei, who conquered China, had a long, reddish beard. Indeed, it was said that people were surprised Kubilai Khan had dark hair and eyes, because most of Genghis Khan's descendants had reddish hair and blue eyes.

Narrated in the *Book of Genesis* of the Old Testament, Noah's ark is said to have rested "on the mountain of Ararat." Some of the nobility of an antediluvian civilization, possibly Atlanteans, may have settled in the Mount Ararat/east Anatolia region (near the countries now known as Armenia and northern Iran). They then moved eastward (to India, Pakistan, etc) and westward (to Central, North and Western Europe), teaching their language (proto Indo-European/Iranian or Aryan), technology (the use of the wheel, domesticated animals, agriculture, etc) and intermixing with the peoples living in those regions.

Like northern India, Germany also was peopled by the Aryans. It should not be thought that Sanskrit is the root, but rather it is but one of the branches of the Aryan world-tree, which was derived from proto-Aryan, like the Germanic languages. Therefore, it shares a common origin and is of the same age as the Germanic languages in which Old Aryan still lives. Wherever the Aryans went, the astrotheological solar-based mysteries went with them and appeared in the course of time, after their origin was forgotten, as the groundwork of religions, epic poems, folk-lore, and nursery tales. (221)

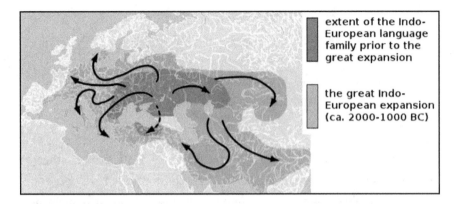

extent of the Indo-
European language
family prior to the
great expansion

the great Indo-
European expansion
(ca. 2000-1000 BC)

FIGURE 49

Almost all that we have of legend comes to us from these ancient Aryan forefathers; sometimes scarcely changed, sometimes so altered that the
links between the old and new have to be puzzled out; but all these myths
and traditions, when we come to know the meaning of them, take us back
to the time when the Aryans dwelt together in the high lands of Central
Asia.(221)

This Aryan expansion included their sea-faring branch the Phoenicians. They were a technologically advanced people who have been mar-
ginalized by official history and this has obscured their true identity. They
are fundamental to understanding where agricultural civilizations emerge,
and what factors contribute to their degradation or downfall. It was they
who brought both their genetic lines and their knowledge to Europe, Scandinavia and the Americas, thousands of years BC. (207)

Chapter 7

We can trace the evolution and spread of the solar-based mysteries and how they became the backbone of all pagan religions. From the Caucasus Mountains region which moved into the Indus Valley of India and created what is today known as the Hindu religion. It was these same Aryan invasions which introduced the ancient Sanskrit language to India and the stories and myths contained in the Hindu holy books, the Vedas. Waddell's research into ancient civilizations established that the father of the first historical Aryan king of India (recorded in the Maha-Barata epic and Indian Buddhist history) was the last historical king of the Hittites in Asia Minor. The Indian Aryans worshiped the Sun as the Father-god Indra, and the Hittite Phoenicians called their Father-god Bel by the name, Indara. Under many names these same Aryan people also settled in Sumer, Babylon, Egypt and Asia Minor, now Turkey, and others, taking with them the same stories, myths, and mystery solar-religion.

This is why all the major religions tell the same tale but using different names. They all come from the same source, this Aryan diffusion during the current Holocene.(207)

Robert Sepehr, Pergamon Museum in Berlin, Germany

FIGURE 63

Teutonic peoples which comes from a term "Teutons," which is a Lati-
nized form of the word meaning the people of Germanic origin in general.
However, it also refers to the languages spoken by other peoples including
the Gothic, Anglo-Saxon, English, Dutch, Icelandic, Norse, Danish, German, and Swedish.

The Cimmerians migrated north west from the Caucasus and Asia Minor (Turkey) into the countries we now call Belgium, the Netherlands, Germany and Denmark. The Roman historians, Pliny and Tacitus, said that all the people along the coast from the Netherlands to Denmark were the same ethnic group and this is supported by archaeological evidence which indicates that this people arrived in that region about 300 to 250 BC. Another group traveled up the River Danube through Hungary and Austria into southern Germany and France. The Romans called them Gauls and the Greeks knew them as the Celts. (207)

The Scythians, another Aryan group, also moved north from the Caucasus into Europe where their name was changed by the Romans to distinguish between them and other peoples. The sacred emblems of the Scythians included the serpent, the Ox (Taurus), fire or flame, Sun, and Tho or Theo; the god the Egyptians called Pan. The Romans called the Scythians the Sarmatae and the Germani from the Latin word Germanus, meaning genuine. (207) Another group of Aryan-Scythians, who became known as the Sakkas, went east from the Caucasus following the trail of the earlier Aryans and they reached the borders of China by 175 BC. About this time Chinese records tell of a people called the Sai-wang or Sok-wang who were forced to flee India. Sok-wang means Sakka princes.

The records indicate that these Sakka retreated south into India through the mountain passes from Afghanistan, and coins dating from about 100 BC confirm that a Sakka kingdom was created in the upper Indus valleys between Kashmir and Afghanistan. Again it is not a coincidence that the religion of Buddhism emerged from lands occupied by the Sakka (Aryan-Scythians). (206, 207)

At least by 500 BC, a tribe called the Sakyas lived in the area where Buddha is supposed to have been born around 63 years earlier. Gautama Buddha was called Sakyashina, Sakamuni, the Sakya sage, Sakya the teacher and the lion of the tribe of Sakya. Sarah Elizabeth Titcomb, in Aryan sun-myths the origin of religions, says that:

In ancient times there lived a noble race of men, called the Aryans. Speaking a language not yet Sanskrit, Greek, or German, but containing the dialects of all, this clan which had advanced to a state of agricultural civilization had recognized the bonds of blood, and sanctioned the bonds of marriage. That they worshiped Nature, the sun, moon, sky and earth. Their chief object of adoration was the sun. Almost all that we have of legend comes to us from our Aryan forefathers, sometimes scarcely changed, sometimes so altered that the links between the old and new have to be puzzled out; but all these myths and traditions, when we come to know the meaning of them, take us back to the time when the Aryans dwelt together in the high lands of Central Asia.(201)

Irish occult historian Michael Tsarion agrees that the Aryan legacy is very ancient and likely antediluvian, pointing to their influence in all parts of the world:

Aryan can be Jew or Gentile, Saxon or Hindu, Celt or Egyptian, Oriental or Nordic, Maya or Maori. Originally, the Aryans were the technically and spiritually endowed Seers, Sages, or Elders of Atlantis.. and the other lost civilizations that flourished and then fell over ten thousand years ago. (220)

These early Aryans worshiped the elements of nature; the Moon, Sky, Earth, and above all the Sun, the ultimate metaphor for "Divine Light". To these people, in the infancy of their newly emerging, post-cataclysmic, civilization, the Sun was not a mere spiritual luminary, but a creator, ruler, and savior of their world as they knew it. As there could be no life or vegetation without light, the Sun, as a light-bringer (literally "Lucifer"), became for these people their creator. In driving away the darkness, likewise in fertilizing the earth, the Sun became for them the preserver/protector or savior of mankind and all liv-

32,000 year old mammoth-ivory sculpture found in 1939 in Germany

FIGURE 64

ing things. As the Sun sometimes scorches and withers vegetation and dries up the rivers, this same Sun was conceived of also as a destroyer. In this context of Creator, Preserver, and Destroyer, the Sun can be seen as a Trinity.

It is to these Vedic hymns written, it is said, from one thousand to fifteen hundred years before the Christian era, that we must go for the development which changes the Sun from a mere luminary into a Supreme Being. These hymns contain the germ-story of the Virgin-born God and Savior, the great benefactor of mankind, who is finally put to death, and rises again to life and immortality on the third day. (219)

In the Sanskrit Dictionary, compiled more than two thousand years ago, we find a full account of the incarnate deity Vishnu, who appeared in

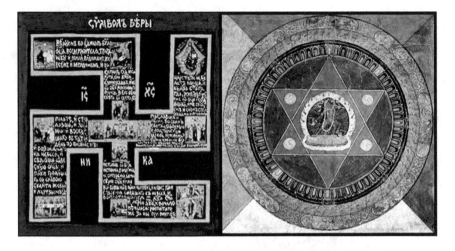

FIGURE 65

human form as Krishna. Vishnu, being moved to relieve the earth of her load of misery and sin, came down from heaven, and was born of the virgin Devaki, on the twenty-fifth of December.(219)

For centuries after the time assigned as the birth of Jesus, he was not represented as a man on a cross. The earliest representation of him was as a lamb.(238) This custom continued until the pontificate of Agathon (a.d. 608), during the reign of Constantine Pogonatus. By the Sixth Synod of Constantinople (Canon 82), it was ordained that instead of the ancient symbol which had been the lamb, the figure of a man nailed to a cross should be represented. All this was confirmed by Pope Adrian I. (203,238)

When discussing nations who are comprehended under the common appellation of Indo-European, Max Muller says:

The Hindus, the Persians, the Celts, Germans, Romans, Greeks, and Slavs - do not only share the same words and the same grammar, slightly modified in each country, but they seem to have likewise preserved a mass of popular traditions which had grown up before they left their common home.(235)

The solar-mysteries, as have been mentioned, went with the Aryans when they peopled Persia, and became the religion of the ancient Parsees. Mithras was the name which the Persians gave to the Sun. After ages had passed, it was utterly forgotten that Mithras was the Sun, and it was believed that he was the Only Begotten Son of God, who had come down from Heaven to be a mediator between God and man, to save men from their sins. The twenty-fifth of December was said to be the day on which this God-man was born, and it was celebrated with great rejoicings.(219)

If we turn to the Egyptians, we find that the Aryan sun-myths became the foundation of their religion also. One of their names for the Sun was Osiris. The facts relating to the incarnation, birth, life, and death of Osiris are very similar to those in the legends of the Hindu and Persian sun-gods. (219)

The sun, moon, and five planets were each of them assigned a day of the week, the seventh day being Saturn's Day, and kept as a holy day. The Immortality of the Soul was believed in and was a very ancient doctrine. (219) Horus, another Egyptian name for the Sun, was said to have been born of the immaculate virgin Isis (the Moon), on the twenty-fifth of December. The ancient Egyptians had the legend of the Tree of Life, the fruit of which enabled those who ate of it to become as gods. (219, 220)

The ancient Greeks had a tradition of the Islands of the Blessed, the Elysium, on the borders of the earth, abounding in every charm of life, and the Garden of the Hesperides, the Paradise, in which grew a tree bearing the golden apples of Immortality. It was guarded by three nymphs and a serpent, or dragon. It was one of the labors of Hercules to gather some of these Apples of Life. Ancient medallions represent a tree with a serpent twined around it. The Greeks, who are Aryans, called themselves the "Hellenes", which means Shining ones, and traced their descent from the people who were destroyed by the Flood, as did other tribes. (220)

The Chinese have a legend of the Sun standing still, and a legend of the Deluge. Accounts of the ascent to Heaven of holy men, without death, are found in their mythology. They believe that in the latter days there will be a millennium, and that a divine man will establish himself on earth, and everywhere restore peace and happiness. From time immemorial the Chinese have worshiped a virgin mother and child. The mother is called

Shin-moo, or the Holy Mother, and is represented with rays of glory sur-rounding her head. Tapers are kept constantly burning before her images, which are elevated in alcoves behind the altars of their temples. (219)

The Mexican sun-god, or savior, Quetzalcoatl, born in the land of Tu-lan in Anahuac, was the son of Tezcatlipoca, the Supreme God of the an-cient Mexicans, and the virgin Sochiquetzal, who was worshiped as the Virgin Mother, the Queen of Heaven. The ancient Mexicans had a tradition of a deluge, from which a person corresponding to Noah was saved, with six others, in an ark, which landed on a mountain, a bird being sent out to ascertain when the waters had subsided. They also had a legend of the building of a tower, which would reach to the skies, their object being to see what was going on in Heaven, and also to have a place of refuge in case of another deluge. The gods beheld with wrath this edifice, the top of which was nearing the clouds, and they hurled fire from heaven upon it, which threw it down and killed many of the workmen. The work was then discon-tinued, as each family interested in the building of the tower received a lan-guage of its own, and the builders could not understand each other. (219)

The Scandinavians worshiped a triune God (a trinity), and consecrated one day in the week to him, the day being called to the present time Odin's, or Woden's day, which is our Wednesday. They observed the rite of Bap-tism. They had a legend of an Eden, or Golden Age, which lasted until the arrival of woman out of Jotunheim, the region of giants.

The ancient Germans worshiped a virgin mother and child. The virgin's name was Ostara, or Eostre, whence comes our Easter. In ancient times this festival was preceded by a week's indulgence in all kinds of sports, called the carnevale.

The worship of the constellation Aries was the worship of the sun in his passage through that sign, and the age was called Aryan. This constellation was called by the ancients the Lamb, or the Ram. On an ancient medal of the Phoe-nicians, brought by Dr. Clark from Citium (and described in his " Travels," vol. ii. ch. xi.), this "Lamb of God " is described with the cross and rosary."

The Phoenix, the mythical bird of Egypt, was in fact the Sun bird of the Phoenicians, the emblem of the Sun God, Bil or Bel, and as it has been later symbolized, a peacock or an eagle.(227)

Chapter 8

Ancient people of various cultures from all over the world seemed to all be very heavily involved in various systems of divination. Whether it be throwing bones, looking at the entrails of animals, gazing into clouds of smoke, the I Ching, reading coffee, tarot cards, astrology, etc, all seem to involve a unique way of linking the human mind, or consciousness, with the very nature of time itself in order to understand cycles of nature and predict the future.

Although they are often overlooked, calendars constitute one of the most important cultural artifacts of human creation. Not only do they order our lives, which is in itself an extremely important function that allows for life on Earth to proceed with regularity, but the study of the history of calendars also reveals the similar zodiacal and common sacred numerical natural cycles interwoven into the occult mysteries of many world religions and shamanistic activities.

Astrotheology is most commonly defined as the study of astronomical influences recorded in religion, implying that religion consists of various astronomical allegories. Astrotheology also represents the observation and reverence of natural cycles and phenomena, including celestial bodies such as the sun, moon, planets, stars, constellations, and their greater potential influence or relevance in our lives. Broadly speaking, however, we can incorporate general nature worship into the definition as well, such that astrotheology could be used to describe the ancient global religion as a whole, which also personified perceived spirits in elements such as wind, water, fire and earth, as well as anthropomorphizing animals, such as the crocodile in Egypt, or the monkey in India. Of course, the main occult attraction that takes center stage in the subject of astrotheology is the veneration of light and it's greatest symbolic representative, the Sun. In the words of researcher and author Jordan Maxwell:

Man's first enemy was darkness. Understanding this one fact alone, people can readily see why the greatest and most trustworthy friend the human race could ever have was by far, heaven's greatest gift to the world... that Glorious Rising Orb of Day: the SUN.

Animals too are affected by the the Sun, as well as the Moon. Hence, the reverence of these celestial bodies, and elements they represent as expressed in numerous sacred celebrations is included in the deeper understanding of astrotheology. This in addition to the many ancient stone structures all over the world, always aligned to the solstices and equinox.

Roughly 12,000 years ago, at the close of the last ice age, a Late Magdalenian tribe settled in southeast Anatolia and built a calendar sanctuary now known as Gobekli Tepe, in what is now modern day Turkey. The oldest known humanoid statue ever discovered at 12,000 years old, referred to as Urfa Man, was also found in the region of Gobekli Tepe. Similar to the blue-eyed statues of ancient Egypt and Sumer, it had dark blue obsidian crystal used for the eyes. Over 5,500 years before the first cities of Mesopotamia, and 7,000 years before the circle of Stonehenge, massive T-shaped stone towers were erected and carved with drawings of lions, scorpions, boars, foxes and other animals. Of the many animals depicted at Gobekli Tepe, the most common species seen is that a snake and representations of it have also been found at other sites.(212)

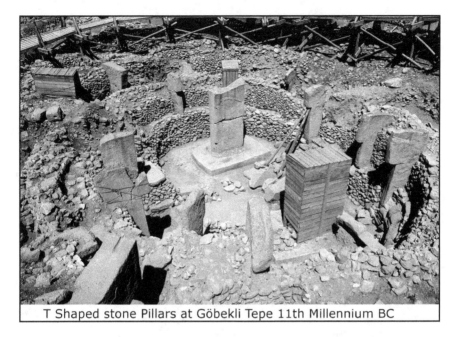

T Shaped stone Pillars at Göbekli Tepe 11th Millennium BC

FIGURE 48

In the center stood what some archeologists have interpreted as a 'Tree of Life', around it large 12 poles, and a zodiac of 12 animals, that symbolized the solar year of a dozen months of 30 days each, a total of 360. We can see the same calendar division of 360 for the solar year used by the Egyptians and Aztec. (212)

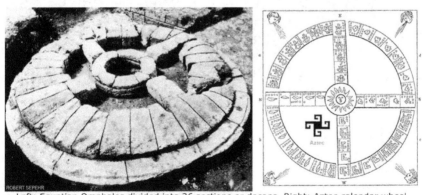

Left: Egyptian Omphalos divided into 36 sections or decans. Right: Aztec calendar wheel outer rim is also divided into 36 sections, plus 4 on each on the inner arms, totalling 52.

FIGURE 57

Based on my own research, and the conclusions of others working in the field (231), it has become exceedingly clear to me that Paleolithic people, specifically those descended from Cro magnon, had been aware of, and continuously tracking, the astronomical phenomenon known as the precession of the equinox since at least the last ice age. (230)

In 1894 the Indian astronomer, Sri Yukteswar (1855–1936), wrote that the cause of the cycle known as precession, or the precession of the equinox, was the result of our sun's orbit around another star. He estimated the orbit period at 24,000 years. This long cycle is the same concept as Plato's Great Year, as well as the Maya Long Count calendar. (214)

Mayan long count calendar

FIGURE 58

The Maya used three different calendars. The first was the sacred calendar, or Tzolk'in, which lasted 260 days and then started over again, just as our 365-day calendar refreshes once it hits Dec. 31. This calendar was important for activities involving agriculture and scheduling religious cer-

136

emonies. The second calendar was the Haab', or secular calendar, which lasted 365 days. The final calendar was the Long Count Calendar, which included dates written out as five hieroglyphs separated by four periods, and recently completed a major cycle. Dec. 21, 2012, on our calendar marked the end of the 13th b'ak'tun of the Mayan Long Count Calendar.

This reverence for the cyclical aspects in nature and time is also present when considering the deeper, occult (hidden), context of the pre-Christian cross, especially in the context of the 4 cardinal points which are of great importance in esoteric astrology and astrotheology. This understanding is the essence behind the symbol most famously referred to as the swastika. Although often considered to have originated in India, the ancient symbol and its meaning was brought into India with the Aryans and predates writ-

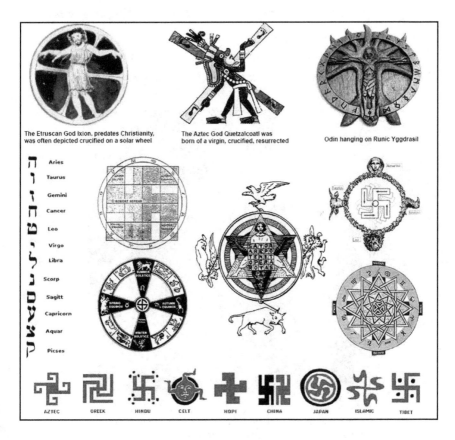

The Etruscan God Ixion, predates Christianity, was often depicted crucified on a solar wheel

The Aztec God Quetzalcoatl was born of a virgin, crucified, resurrected

Odin hanging on Runic Yggdrasil

FIGURE 59

ten Sanskrit itself, which was also introduced to India. In fact, these same Aryans introduced the horse and chariot to India, which are mentioned in the ancient Aryan epics of India. The Aryan invasion theory has become politically incorrect in recent years, as egalitarianism is painted over a colonialist history. That said, the caste system which is still visible in India today, was imposed by these same Aryans, which accord to some Indian nationalists, are fabricated stories of people who never invaded.

One of the interpretations of the swastika is as an emblem of the solar year, as well as Plato's "Great Year", which is also know as the precession of the equinox. The ancient Greeks associated the Swastika symbol with the sun god Apollo, exemplifying the symbol's historic and universal use as a solar emblem.

The Fixed Cross, consisting of the four constellations, has the same four signs regarded in the Christian belief as the four living creatures of the prophet Ezekiel. These four had the face of a man, Aquarius; the body of a lion, Leo; the horns of an ox, Taurus; and the wings of an eagle, Scorpio. The Eagle, incidentally, was astrologically interchangeable with Scorpio.

The Face of a Man, Aquarius; The Body of a Lion, Leo
The Horns of an Ox, Taurus; The Wings of an Eagle, Scorpio
(The Eagle was astrologically interchangeable with Scorpio)

FIGURE 66

138

Human (Aquarius), Lion (Leo), Bull (Taurus), Eagle (Scorpio)

FIGURE 67

These same 4 fixed signs of the zodiac are symbolized in the four evangelists, and in the four beasts of Revelations. Keep in mind that Scorpio has not just two symbols but three: the Scorpion, the Eagle and the Phoenix.

The Worship of the Golden Calf
by Filippino Lippi (1457–1504)

"Moses Breaking the Tables of the Law"
Exo 32:19 ...he saw the calf, and the dancing: and Moses'
anger waxed hot, and he cast the tables out of his hands,
and brake them beneath the mount.

FIGURE 68

When Moses was said to have descended from the mountain with the ten commandments (17th - 13th century BC, the end of the Age of Taurus), some of his people or followers were found by him to be worshiping a golden bull calf. He instructed these worshipers to be killed. This represents Moses "killing" the bull, ending the Age of Taurus, and ushering in the Age of Aries; which he represents when he is depicted with ram horns.

This is the same scenario when Mithras, as the solar hero/deity, ends the Taurean Age by killing the Bull, ushering in the Aryan age. This ancient ritual is still played out with bullfighting today, and the reason why the bullfighter with the red solar cape (Bulls are color-blind to red) traditionally ends up killing the bull at the end.

White marble relief with Mithras slaying bull

FIGURE 60

In Egypt, and in civilizations of the Americas, we find the worship of a sun god. In Egypt the sun god was called Ra. The Toltec of Mexico called their sun god Rana and the Peruvian sun god was Raymi. Carl G. Jung said:

◇◇

"The sun is actually the only reasonable symbol for god. The sun is the father god who gives life to all appearances, the creator of all living things, the energy source of our world."

◇◇

The Egyptian legends refer to a time when the sun was completely obscured in dense clouds. The ancient Egyptians also relate to "ages of fire and ice, and the victory of the sun-god over the evil-one". During the time of fire and ice, there is also mention of a "cave-life", a time when people lived in mountain caves to escape the devastation. (215)

Most all of the civilizations in South/Central America and Egypt preserved a tradition of a deluge. As we often see in Flood mythology, there is the transfer of the Atlantis legend by an Atlantean people to a high mountain in their new home. In *Timaeus*, Plato recounts the tale told from the Egyptian priests:

◇◇

There have been, and will be again, many destructions of mankind arising out of many causes; the greatest have been brought about by the agencies of fire and water, and other lesser ones by innumerable other causes. There is a story, which even you have preserved, that once upon a time Phaethon, the son of Helios, having yoked the steeds in his father's chariot, because he was not able to drive them in the path of his father, burnt up all that was upon the earth, and was himself destroyed by a thunderbolt. Now this has the form of a myth, but really signifies a declination of the bodies moving in the heavens around the earth, and a great conflagration of things upon the earth, which recurs after long intervals.(233)

◇◇

The Egyptian priests, via Plato, point out that the ancient myth clearly refers to celestial events, and the perceived alterations that come about when changes happen at regular periodic intervals. It is explained to Solon, the Greek statesman, that his people lack records of these events because they are so devastating that even language and writing itself can be lost. The priest continues:

◇◇

Whereas just when you and other nations are beginning to be provided with letters and the other requisites of civilized life, after the
usual interval, the stream from heaven, like a pestilence, comes
pouring down, and leaves only those of you who are destitute of
letters and education; and so you have to begin all over again like
children, and know nothing of what happened in ancient times,
either among us or among yourselves. In the first place you remember a single deluge only, but there were many previous ones;
in the next place, you do not know that there formerly dwelt in
your land the fairest and noblest race of men which ever lived, and
that you and your whole city are descended from a small seed or
remnant of them which survived. And this was unknown to you,
because, for many generations, the survivors of that destruction
died, leaving no written word.(233)

◇◇

What celestial bodies could influence cataclysmic events on earth?
NASA scientists are searching for an invisible "Death Star" that is hypothesized to circle our Sun and periodically catapult potentially cata-
strophic comets at the Earth. The theoretical star, also known to Astronomers as Nemesis, is expected to exceed five times the size of Jupiter
and could be to blame for the impact that wiped out the dinosaurs 65
million years ago. The bombardment of celestial missiles is being blamed
by some scientists for mass extinctions of life that they say happen periodically on Earth.

Some scientists believe that Nemesis is a red or brown dwarf; a "failed
star" that has not managed to generate enough energy to burn like the Sun.
It may eventually be detectable by the super heat-sensitive space telescope
called WISE, the Wide-Field Infrared Survey Explorer, but so far nothing
has been officially admitted to to the public.

Our solar system is thought to be surrounded by a vast sphere of distant bodies called the Oort cloud. Some of this space debris may get kicked in towards the inner planets as comets; giant snowballs of ice, dust and rock. The suggestion is that the "Death Star's" massive gravitational influence is to blame. Paleontologists David Raup and Jack Sepkoski discovered that, over the last 250 million years, life on Earth has been devastated on a fairly regular and predictable cycle. Comet impacts are suggested as a likely cause for these periodic global catastrophes.

Most stars have one or more companion stars orbiting around each other, which would make the sun's single status unusual. A major clue to Nemesis's existence is a mysterious dwarf planet called Sedna that was spotted on an elongated 12,000-year-long orbit around the sun. Mike Brown, who discovered Sedna, said:

Sedna is a very odd object, it shouldn't be there! It never comes anywhere close to any of the giant planets or the sun. It's way, way out there on this incredibly eccentric orbit. The only way to get on an eccentric orbit is to have some giant body kick you, so what is out there?

Professor John Matese, of the University of Louisiana, says most comets in the inner solar system seem to come from the same region of the Oort Cloud, launched by the pull of a companion star to the sun that scatters comets in its wake. He suggests it is up to five times the size of Jupiter, adding that: "There is statistically significant evidence that this concentration of comets could be caused by a companion to the Sun."

Whatever the cause of these periodic cataclysms on earth, it is clear is that there was a massive event that separates the Pleistocene (ice age) from our current Holocene age roughly 11,500 years ago. Rapidly melting ice caps caused a global rise in sea levels, submerging island and coastal communities world wide. Once we confront this, we may discover our historic cradle of civilization was never out-of-Africa, but out-of-Aftantis.

Bibliography

1.   *The New York Times,* (November 21-23, 1953)

2.   Scott, Dave. *Icon of Evolution 'Lucy' Bites the Dust.* (2007)

3.   Stokstad, E. *Hominid Ancestors May Have Knuckle Walked.* Science. 287:2131-2132. (2000).

4.   Richmond; Strait. *Evidence that Humans Evolved from Knuckle-Walking Ancestor.* Nature; Vol. 404. (3/23/2000).

5.   Gish, Dr. Duane. *Evolution: The Fossils Still Say No.* Institute for Creation Research. (1985).

6.   Berge, Christine. *How did the australopithecines walk? A biomechanical study of the hip and thigh of Australopithecus afarensis.* Journal of Human Evolution. (1994).

7.   Roger Lewin, *Bones of Contention.* p. 164 (1987)

8.   Oxnard, Charles. *The Order of Man: A Biomathematical Anatomy of the Primates.* Yale Press. (1984).

9.   *The New York Times.* (Aug. 29, 2009)

10. Darwin, Charles. *The Descent of Man.* D. Appleton and Company. (1871)

11. Green, D. and Alemseged, Z. "Australopithecus afarensis Scapular Ontogeny, Function, and the Role of Climbing in Human Evolution", Science 338. (October 2012)

12. de Camp, L. Sprague. *The Great Monkey Trial.* Doubleday. (1968).

13. Conkin, Paul K.. *When All the Gods Trembled: Darwinism, Scopes, and American Intellectuals.* Rowman & Littlefield Publishers, Inc. (1998).

14. Folsom, Burton W. Jr. *The Scopes Trial Reconsidered.* Continuity (1988).

15. Larson, Edward J. *Summer for the Gods: The Scopes Trial and America's Continuing Debate Over Science and Religion*. BasicBooks. (1997).

16. Huse, Scott M. *The Collapse of Evolution*. Baker Book House, page 135. (1997).

17. *Time* Magazine. (January 10, 1927)

18. *Time* Magazine. *The Diggers*. (August 15, 1927)

19. New York Times. *Human tooth found in Montana coal bed*. Page 3. (November 8, 1926)

20. Johanson, Donald C.; Wong, Kate. *Lucy's Legacy: The Quest for Human Origins*. Crown Publishing. (2010).

21. *Mother of man - 3.2 million years ago*. BBC Home. (2008).

22. Comninellis, Nicholas; White, Joe. *Darwin's Demise: Why Evolution Can't Take the Heat*. Master books. (2001).

23. Darwin, Charles. *On the Origin of Species*. (1859).

24. Barras, Colin. "Baboon bone found in famous Lucy skeleton". New Scientist. (April 2015).

25. McKie, Robin. *Piltdown Man: British archaeology's greatest hoax*. The Guardian Observer. (February 2012).

26. Gould, Stephen J. *The Panda's Thumb*, W. W. Norton and Co. pp. 108–124, ISBN 0-393-01380-4 (1980).

27. Gregory, W.K. *Hesperopithecus apparently not an ape nor a man*. Science 66 (1720): 579–81. (1927).

28. Gibbons, Ann. *A new kind of ancestor: Ardipithecus unveiled*. Science 326 (5949): 36–40. (October 2009).

29. Lachance, Joseph et al. "Evolutionary History and Adaptation from High-Coverage Whole-Genome Sequences of Diverse African Hunter-Gatherers", Cell, Vol. 150 , Issue 3 . (2012).

30. Green, R. E. et al Science 328, 71022. (2010).

31. ncbi.nlm.nih.gov/pubmed/20448178?dopt=Abstract&holding=npg

32. Meyer, M., "A high-coverage genome sequence from an archaic Denisovan individual", Science 338, (2012)

33. Georgiev O, et al., "A recent evolutionary change affects a regulatory element in the human FOXP2 gene", (2012)

34. Klyosov, A. & Rozhanskii, I. "Re-Examining the "Out of Africa" Theory and the Origin of Europeoids (Caucasoids) in Light of DNA Genealogy", Advances in Anthropology, 2, 80-86. (2012).

35. Klyosov, A. & Rozhanskii, I. Re-Examining the "Out of Africa" Theory and the Origin of Europeoids (Caucasoids) in Light of DNA Genealogy. Advances in Anthropology, 2, 80-86. doi: 10.4236/ aa.2012.22009. (2012).

36. https://web.stanford.edu/group/stanfordbirds/text/essays/Hybridization.html

37. Seguin, Andaine. "Genomic structure in Europeans dating back at least 36,200 years". Science, (2014)

38. Leonard, R.C. *Atlantis and Cro-Magnon Man, Anthropological Insights.* (2011)

39. Coon, Carleton S., *The Races of Europe*, Macmillan, New York, (1939)

40. Bordes, Francois, *The Old Stone Age*, McGraw-Hill Book Co., New York, (1968)

41. Pfeiffer, John E., *The Emergence of Man.* Harper & Row, New York & London. (1969)

42. Hawkes, Jacquetta. *The Atlas of Early Man.* New York: St. Martin's Press. 1976

43. Hibben, Frank C., *Prehistoric Man in Europe*, Oklahoma University Press, Norman, (1958)

44. Briggs, L. Cabot, *The Stone Age Races of Northwest Africa*, Bulletin of the American School of Prehistoric Research, No. 18, Cambridge, (1955).

45. Torres, M.J.F., *Biological and archaeological information in coprolites from an early site in Patagonia*, Current Research in the Pleistocene, Vol. iii, Nos. 74-75, (1986).

46. Charroux, Robert, *One Hundred Thousand Years of Man's Unknown History*. (translated from the French by Lowell Bair), Berkley Publ. Corp., (1970).

47. Campbell, Duncan. *Bad karma for cross llama without a hump.* (2002)

48. Liliana Cortez-Ortiz, Thomas F. Duda, Jr., "Hybridization in Large-Bodied New World Primates", Genetics, (August 2007)

49. Kelaita, M. A. and Cortez-Ortiz, L., "Morphological variation of genetically confirmed Alouatta Pigra A. palliata hybrids from a natural hybrid zone in Tabasco, Mexico". Am. J. Phys. Anthropol. (2013)

50. "The Race Question", UNESCO, (1950)

51. Hammer, M.F.; Woerner, A.E.; Mendez, F.L.; Watkins, J.C.; Wall, J.D. "Genetic evidence for archaic admixture in Africa". Proceedings of the National Academy of Sciences. (2011).

52. Lachance, J.; et al. "Evolutionary History and Adaptation from High-Coverage Whole-Genome Sequences of Diverse African Hunter-Gatherers". Cell. (2012).

53. Callaway, E. "Hunter-gatherer genomes a trove of genetic diversity". Nature. (26 July 2012).

54. Stringer, C. "What makes a modern human". Nature 485 (7396): 33–35.(2012).

55. Green, R.E.; Krause, J.; Briggs, A.W.; Maricic, T.; Stenzel, U.; Kircher, M. et al. "A Draft Sequence of the Neandertal Genome". Science 328 (5979): 710–722. (2010).

56. Prüfer, K.; Racimo, F.; Patterson, N.; Jay, F.; Sankararaman, S.; Sawyer, S. et al. "The complete genome sequence of a Neanderthal from the Altai Mountains". Nature 505 (7481): 43–49. (2014)

57. Sankararaman, S.; Patterson, N.; Li, H.; Pääbo, S.; Reich, D; Akey, J.M. "The Date of Interbreeding between Neandertals and Modern Humans". PLoS Genetics 8 (10): e1002947.(2012).

58. Meyer, M.; Kircher, M.; Gansauge, M.T.; Li, H.; Racimo, F.; Mallick, S. et al. "A High-Coverage Genome Sequence from an Archaic Denisovan Individual". Science 338 (6104): 222–226 (2012).

59. Wall, J.D. et al. "Higher Levels of Neanderthal Ancestry in East Asians than in Europeans". Genetics 194 (1): 199–209. (2013)

60. Sankararaman, S.; et al. "Te genomic landscape of Neanderthal ancestry in present-day humans". Nature 507 (7492): 354–357. (2014).

61. Lowery, R.K.; et al. "Neanderthal and Denisova genetic affinities with contemporary humans: Introgression versus common ancestral polymorphisms". Gene 530 (1): 83–94. (2013).

62. Bowman, J.; Chown, B.; Lewis, M.; Pollock, J. M. "Rh-immunization during pregnancy: antenatal prophylaxis". Canadian Med Ass Journal. (1978).

63. Scott ML (2004). "The complexities of the Rh system". Vox

64. "It's The Frankenstein Monster Of The Fish World: The Blood Parrot!". AquaFriend.com. (2002)

65. Bataagiin Bynie: Mongolia: The Country Refort (sic!) On Animal Genetic Resources, Ulaanbaatar p. 11 (2002)

66. "Meet Rama the cama... BBC". BBC News. (1998-01-21).

67. James Mallet. "Hybridization, ecological races and the nature of species: empirical evidence for the ease of speciation". (2008).

68. Wilson, P. J. "DNA profiles of the eastern Canadian wolf and the red wolf provide evidence for a common evolutionary history independent of the gray wolf". Canadian Journal of Zoology. (2000).

69. "Blast from the Past. The Very First F1 Savannah". Feline Conservation Federation (2007)

70. Carroll, Sean B. "Remarkable creatures". New York Times. (September 13, 2010).

71. Sanford, Malcolm T. "The Africanized Honey Bee in the Americas: A Biological Revolution with Human Cultural Implications". American Bee Journal. (2006).

72. Guynup, Sharon. "The mating game: ligers, zorses, wholphins, and other hybrid animals raise a beastly science question: what is a species?" missouri.edu

73. Steven Strong, Andy Whiteley, "DNA Evidence Debunks the "Out-of-Africa" Theory of Human Evolution", Wake Up World. (2013)

74. Walker, D. N.; Frison, G. C. "Studies on Amerindian Dogs 3: Prehistoric Wolf/Dog Hybrids from the Northwestern Plains". Journal of Archaeological Science. (1982).

75. Miller, Crichton. *The Golden Thread of Time*. (2000)

76. Leonard, R. Cedric. *Atlantis and Cro-Magnon Man*, (2011)

77. Burenhult, Goran, *People of the Stone Age*, from: The Illustrated History of Humankind Vol. 2, Landmark Series of the American Museum of Natural History, Harper-Collins, (1993).

78. Mary A. Kelaital, Liliana Cortés-Ortiz, "Morphological variation of genetically confirmed Alouatta Pigra × A. palliata hybrids from a natural hybrid zone in Tabasco, Mexico", American Journal of Physical Anthropology Volume 150, Issue 2, (February 2013)

79. Bordes, Francois, *The Old Stone Age*, McGraw-Hill Book Co., New York, (1968).

80. Daily Mail. "Ancient humans 'rampantly interbred' with Neanderthals and a mystery species in Lord Of The Rings-style world of different creatures". *(19 November 2013)*

81. Hammer, Michael. "Out of Africa and Back Again: Nested Cladistic Analysis of Human Y Chromosome Variation", (1998)

82. F.E Grine, et al., "Late Pleistocene Human Skull from Hofmeyr, South Africa, and Modern Human Origins", Science (12 January 2007)

83. Pengfei Qin, Mark Stoneking, "Denisovan Ancestry in East Eurasian and Native American Populations". (2015)

84. Prufer et al., "The complete genome sequence of a Neanderthal from the Altai Mountains". Nature. (2014).

85. Nature, *Sequence variants in SLC16A11 are a common risk factor for type 2 diabetes in Mexico*

86. Encyclopedia Britannica 1994-2002

87. Hammer, M.F.; et al. "Genetic evidence for archaic admixture in Africa". Proceedings of the National Academy of Sciences. (2011).

88. Lachance, J.; et al. "Evolutionary History and Adaptation from High-Coverage Whole-Genome Sequences of Diverse African Hunter-Gatherers". Cell 150. (2012)

89. F.E. Grine et al., "Late Pleistocene Human Skull from Hofmeyr, South Africa, and Modern Human Origins", (2007)

90. Marshack, Alexander. *Lunar Notation of Upper Paleolithic Remains*. Science. (1964).

91. Spence, Lewis T. *The History of Atlantis*, Rider & Co., London. 1926.

92. Thorndike, Joseph J. Jr. *Mysteries of the Past*. American Heritage, New York. 1977.

93. Hadingham, Evan. *Secrets of the Ice Age*. Walker and Company, New York. (1979).

94. Smith, Philip E. L. "Stone Age Man on the Nile. Scientific American", Vol. 235. (1976).

95. Allers K, Hütter G, Hofmann J, Loddenkemper C, Rieger K, Thiel E et al. "Evidence for the cure of HIV infection by CCR5Δ32/Δ32 stem cell transplantation". Blood 117 (10): 2791–9. (2011).

96. Jegues-Wolkiewiez, Chantal. *Etoiles dans la nuit des temps.* HAR-MATTAN. (2000)

97. "The roots of astronomy, or the hidden order of a Palaeolithic work" (in Les Antiquités Nationales, tome 37 pages 43 - 52), February 2007.

98. Caramelli et al. "A 28,000 Years Old Cro-Magnon mtDNA Sequence Differs from All Potentially Contaminating Modern Sequences." PLoS One, (2008)

99. Sepehr, Robert. *1666 Redemption Through Sin. Global Conspiracy in History, Religion, Politics and Finance* Atlantean Gardens. (2015)

100. Sepehr, Robert. *Occult Secrets of Vril, Goddess Energy and Human Potential.* Atlantean Gardens. (2015)

101. Donnelly, Ignatius. *Atlantis, Antediluvian World.* (1882)

102. Plato. *Timaeus* (360 B.C.E.)

103. Hall,Manly P. *Secret Teachings of the Ages.* (1928)

104. Leonard, R. Cedric. "Pre-Platonic Writings Pertinent to Atlantis" (2008)

105. Pratt, David. *The Ancient Americas: migrations, contacts, and Atlantis.* (2009)

106. Weber, George. *Clovis people (New Mexico, USA) and Minnesota Woman.* Minnesota, USA. (2008)

107. Leonard, R. Cedric. *Atlanteans in America: Paleolithic Cro-Magnons in America.* (2008)

108. Patterson, Nice. et al. "Ancient Admixture in Human History", Genetics. Volume 192, (November 2012).

109. Andrews, Shirley. *Atlantis: insights from a lost civilization.* (2002)

110. Brown, Wallace, et al., American Journal of Human Genetics, University of Chicago Press (1998)

111. Am J, Hum Genet. *mtDNA haplogroup X: An ancient link between Europe/Western Asia and North America? (1998)*

112. Ripan S. Malhi and David Glenn Smith, *Brief Communication: Haplogroup X Confirmed in Prehistoric North America*

113. Lindsay, Jeff. *Y Chromosome Haplogroups 4 and 1C and mtDNA Haplogroup X*

114. Little, Gregory L., Van Auken, John, Little, Lora. *Ancient South America*. P 50. (2002)

115. Kurlansky, Mark. *The Basque History of the World*. Random House Publ., New York. (2001)

116. Alexander Braghine, Shadow of Atlantis, 1940, p. 187-188

117. Louis Farrar, A Modern Survival of Ancient Linguistics, 1922

118. Muck, Otto. *The Secret of Atlantis*. (1954)

119. Ryan, Pittman. *Noah's Flood. The New Scientific Discoveries about the Event that Changed History*. (1998)

120. Center for Basque Studies University of Nevada, Reno, Nevada 89557-2322

121. von Humboldt, Wilhelm. *Researches into the Early Inhabitants of Spain with the help of the Basque language* (original title: Prüfung der Untersuchungen über die Urbewohner Hispaniens vermittelst der vaskischen Sprache), (1821)

122. Blanc, S. H., *Grammaire de la Langue Basque* (d'apres celle de Larramendi), Lyons & Paris. (1854)

123. Ripley, William Z., *The Races of Europe*. D. Appleton & Co., New York, (1899)

124. Hiernaux, Jean, *The People of Africa*, Charles Schribner's Sons, New York, (1975)

125. Leonard, R. Cedric. *A Paleolithic Language*. (2011)

126. Lundman, Bertil J., *The Races and Peoples of Europe*, IAAEE Monograph No. 4 (translated from German by Donald A. Swan), New York, (1977)

127. Harrison, Michael. *The Roots of Witchcraft*. Citadel Press, Secaucas, N.J. (1974)

128. Conrado Rodriguez-Martín. *Mummies, Disease, and Ancient Cultures*. Cambridge University Press. (1998)

129. Professor Retzius, "Smithsonian Report," p. 266 (1859)

130. Blavatsky, H.P., *The Secret Doctrine*. Theosophical University Press. (1888)

131. Kapnistos, Peter Fotis. "More Terrible than Atlantis?"

132. Encyclopaedia Britannica 11th ed. 1911

133. Baumgarten, Albert Irwin. *The Phoenician History of Philo of Byblos: a Commentary*. Leiden: E. J. Brill. (1981)

134. Fremantle, Francesca. *Luminous Emptiness: understanding the Tibetan Book of the Dead*. Shambhala Publications (2001)

135. Verbrugghe, Gerald P., and John Moore Wickersham. Berossos and Manetho, Introduced and Translated: Native Traditions in Ancient Mesopotamia and Egypt. Ann Arbor: University of Michigan Press. (1996)

136. Leonard, R. Cedric. "PREDYNASTIC EGYPT: The Archeological Story" (2008)

137. Bible, King James translation of 1611. The Greek LXX Version, Zondervan Publ. House, Grand Rapids, (1970)

138. Plato, *Critias*, (360 B.C.E.)

139. Wallace DC et al. "Mitochondrial DNA variation in human evolution and disease". NCBI. (1999)

140. Stanton, G.R. *Athenian Politics c800–500BC: A Sourcebook*, Routledge, London (1990)

141. Brown MD, et al., "mtDNA haplogroup X: An ancient link between Europe/Western Asia and North America", (1998)

142. Karafet TM, et al., "Ancestral Asian source(s) of new world Y-chromosome founder haplotypes", (1999)

143. François Hammer 1 and Nicolas Gruel, "Jewish and Middle Eastern non-Jewish populations share a common pool of Y-chromosome biallelic haplotypes", (2000)

144. Edgar Cayce, Hugh Lynn Cayce. *Edgar Cayce on Atlantis* (1962)

145. Scientific American, November 1991, pages 104-105.

146. Elizabeth S Brown, "Distribution of the ABO and rhesus (D) blood groups in the north of Scotland" (1965)

147. Barry Fell, "America B.C.: Ancient Settlers in the New World", (1989)

148. Willoughby, C.C. 1935. Antiquities of the New England Indians. Peabody Museum Publications.

149. Stone AC, Stoneking M. 1998. mtDNA analysis of a prehistoric One-ota population: implications for the peopling of the New World. Am J Hum Genet 62:1153–1170.

150. Hauswirth WW, Dickel CD, Rowold DJ, Hauswirth MA. 1994. Inter- and intrapopulation studies of ancient humans. Experientia 50:585–591.

151. Ribeiro-Dos-Santos AKC et al. 1996. Heterogeneity of mitochondrial DNA haplotypes in pre-Columbian natives of the Amazon region. Am J Phys Anthropol 101:29–37.

152. Royce, Mbel. 1976. *Blood of the Gods.*

153. Webb, Stuart. 2012. *Atlantis and Other Lost Worlds.* Paranormal Files.

154. Hiram Bingham, *Across South America; an account of a journey from Buenos Aires to Lima by way of Potosí, Boston, NY*: Houghton Mifflin Company, p. 277 (1911)

155. Fawcett, Col. P.H. *Exploration Fawcett*, (1953), pp. 75-7

156. Protzen,Jean-Pierre. *Inca Architecture and Construction at Ollantay-tambo*, p. 187. (1993)

157. Perez, Juanjo. *Los ablandadores de piedras*, (Sep 2006,)

158. Protzen, Jeane-Pierre. *Inca Architecture and Construction at Ollan-taytambo*, pp. 170-1 (1993)

159. Maurice Cotterell, *The Lost Tomb of Viracocha: Unlocking the secrets of the Peruvian pyramids*, London: Headline, (2001) p. 67.

160. Donnelly, I. *Atlantis: The Antediluvian World. New York: Gramercy Publishing Company.* (1982)

161. Donnelly, I. Ragnarok: The age of fire and gravel. New York: University Books. (1949)

162. Hammond, N. *The emergence of Mayan civilization. Scientific American*, pp. 106-115. (1985, August).

163. Toth, M., & Nielsen, G. *Pyramid Power.* New York: Destiny Books. (1985).

164. Cayce, E. E. *Edgar Cayce on Atlantis.* New York: Paperback Library. (1969).

165. Dan Vergano, USA TODAY, "Discovery could bring Peru's 'cloud warriors' to earth", (Jan 2007)

166. Titcomb, Sarah Elizabeth. *Aryan sun-myths the origin of religions* (1889)

167. Dottie Indyke. *The History of an Ancient Human Symbol.* (2005.)

168. Origin of Caucasoid-Specific Mitochondrial DNA Lineages in the Ethnic Groups of the Altaiayan Region M. V. Derenko, B. A. Malyarchuk and I. A. Zakharov, (2002)

169. Bouakaze et al, First successful assay of Y-SNP typing by SNaPshot minisequencing on ancient DNA, International Journal of Legal Medicine, vol 121 (2007), pp. 493-499.

170. Keyser et al, Ancient DNA provides new insights into the history of South Siberian Kurgan people, Human Genetics, vol. 125, no. 3 (September 2009), pp. 395-410.

171. Lalueza-Fox et al, "Unraveling migrations in the steppe: mitochondrial DNA sequences from ancient central Asians" (2004)

172. Langmead, Ben. "Frontiers of Sequencing Data Analysis" (2014)

173. Keith, Arthur. *Ur Excavations* (1927)

174. Darius the Great, "Behistun Inscription" (522 BC)

175. Anthology of the Patriarchal Hall (952)

176. *Pali Canon* (29 BC)

177. Dr. Han Kangxin, Physical Anthropologist at the Institute of Archeology in Beijing

178. Coppens, Philip. *White Masters in the deserts of China*, New Dawn, Volume 10, Number 12 (2009)

179. Blavatsky, H.P. *The Secret Doctrine* (1888)

180. Coppens, Philip. *White Masters in the deserts of China*, New Dawn, Volume 10, Number 12 (2009)

181. von Hagen, Adriana. "An Overview of Chachapoya Archaeology and History" Museo Leymebamba

182. Muscutt, Keith. *Warriors of the Clouds.* University of New Mexico Press, Albuquerque, (1998)

183. J. Marla Toyne, *Tibial surgery in ancient Peru*, University of Central Florida, Orlando, FL, USA (2014)

184. Giffhorn, Hans. *Was America Discovered in Ancient Times?* (2013, 2014). Published in the German Language as *Wurde Amerika in der Antike entdeckt? Karthager, Kelten und das Rätsel der Chachapoya*

185. Vergano, Dan. "Discovery could bring Peru's 'cloud warriors' to earth", USA TODAY (Jan 2007)

186. Heyerdahl, Thor. *The Kon-Tiki Expedition: By Raft Across the South Seas* (1948)

187. Heyerdahl, Thor. *The Bearded Gods Speak.* (1971)

188. Cotterell, Maurice. *The Lost Tomb of Viracocha: Unlocking the Secrets of the Peruvian Pyramids.* (2003)

189. "The Mystery of China's Celtic Mummies". *The Independent.* (2006)

190. Mair, Victor H., "Mummies of the Tarim Basin," Archaeology, vol. 48, no. 2 (1995)

191. Chunxiang Li, et al. "Evidence that a West-East admixed population lived in the Tarim Basin as early as the early Bronze Age". BMC Biology (2010)

192. Barber, Elizabeth Wayland. "The Mummies of Ürümchi"

193. Adams, R. E. W. Rio Azul. National Geographic, pp. 420-449 (1986, April)

194. Wilson, Thomas. *The Swastika: The Earliest Known Symbol and its Migrations*. (1896)

195. von Schwerin, H. *Nordic Elements in Afro-Asia*. Northern World IV (2) pp. 24-30. (1960).

196. von Schwerin, H. *European Elements in Afro-Asia*. Mankind Quarterly IV pp. 127-133. (1964)

197. Guillaume, A. *The Life of Muhammad: A Translation of Ibn Hisham's "Sirat Rasul Allah"*. Oxford: University Press.(1987)

198. Baltzer, H. Rasse und Kultur: *Ein Gang durch die Weltgeschichte*. (Weimar: Duncker Verlag). (1934)

199. Lewis, B. *Race and Slavery in the Middle East: An Historical Enquiry*. Oxford: University Press. (1990)

200. Vollers, K. *Über Rassenfarben in der arabischen Literatur*. Siragusa. (1910)

201. Günther, H. F. K. *Rassenkunde des jüdischen Volkes*. Munich: J. F. Lehmans Verlag. (1930)

202. Grant, M. *Dawn of the Middle Ages*. Weidenfeld & Nicolson. (1981)

203. Coon, C.S. *The Races of Europe*. Macmillan. (1939)

204. Sordo, E. [I. Michae, trans.] Moorish Spain: Cordoba, Seville, Granada (New York: Crown Publishers). (1962)

205. Payne, S. G. A History of Spain and Portugal: Volume One (Madison: University of Wisconsin Press). (1973)

206. Fossier, R. "The Beginning of Europe's Expansion." In Dunan & Bowle pp. 298-321. (1968)

207. Günther, H. F. K. [G. C. Wheeler, trans.] The Racial Elements of European History (London: Methuen). (1927)

208. Weyl, N. "The Arab World: A Study of Biogenetic Disintegration." Mankind Quarterly VIII pp. 26-43. (1967)

209. Baltzer, H. Rasse und Kultur: Ein Gang durch die Weltgeschichte (Weimar: Duncker Verlag).(1934)

210. Günther, H. F. K. Die nordische Rasse bei den Indogermanen Asiens (Munich). (1934)

211. Gayre of Gayre, R. *Miscellaneous Racial Studies*, 1943-1972: Volume II (Edinburgh: Armorial).(1972)

212. http://almashriq.hiof.no/turkey/900/950/956/sultans/thumbnails.html

213. *Origin of Caucasoid-Specific Mitochondrial DNA Lineages in the Ethnic Groups of the Altai–Sayan Region* M. V. Derenko, B. A. Malyarchuk and I. A. Zakharov, (2002)

214. Howard-Carter, "The Tangible Evidence for the Earliest Dilmun," Journal of Cuneiform Studies. (1981)

215. *Enmerkar*, lines 25-87, pp. 113-16; lines 124-27, p. 118; lines 196-205, pp. 121-22; lines 281-93

216. S. N. Kramer, Sumerians, pp. 272-73.

217. Donnelly, Ignatious. 1882. *Atlantis the Antediluvian World.*

218. Laurence Gardner; Genesis of the Grail Kings, 2001

219. Titcomb, Sarah Elizabeth, Aryan sun-myths the origin of religions; (1889)

220. Tsarion, Michael. *The Irish Origins of Civilization, Volume 1.* Taroscopes (2007)

221. Morris, Charles. *The Aryan Race: its Origin and its Achievements.* Chicago. (1889)

222. Indyke, Dottie. *The History of an Ancient Human Symbol.* (2005)

223. Royal Saskatchewan Museum. 2445 Albert St, Regina, SK S4P 4W7, Canada

224. The Official City Website for Albuquerque, New Mexico

225. Icke, David. *The Biggest Secret.* (1993)

226. Wadell, L.A. *The Phoenician Origins Of Britons,* p 48 (1924)

227. Dupuis's Origin of Religious Belief p. 252 ; also Higgins's Anacalypsis, Vol. II. p. 3

228. Whitney, William Dwight. *Oriental and Linguistic Studies: The Veda; The Avesta; The Science of Language.* London. (1874)

229. Gnaedinger, Franz. *Very Early Calendars.* (2005)

230. Jègues-Wolkiewiez, Chantal. *Sur les chemins étoilés de Lascaux.* La Pierre Philosophale (2011)

231. Giri, Sri Yukteswar. *The Holy Science.* Kaivalya Darsanam (1894)

232. Donelly, Ignatious. *Ragnarok: The Age of Fire and Gravel.* University Books. (1970)

233. Plato. *Timaeus.* (360 BC)

234. Jameson, Anna. *History of our Lord in Art,* Vol. I. (1864)

235. Müller, Friedrich Max. *India: What Can It Teach Us?: A Course of Lectures Delivered Before the University of Cambridge.* Longmans, Green. (1883)

236. Imam Gazzali. *Mysteries of Cleanliness.* From Revival of Religious Learnings DATE: 450 (A.H.) 1058 A.D.- 505 A.H. 1111 A.D. Translated by Fazlul Karim Published by Darul Ishaat Karachi Parkistan

237. von Schwerin, Henric. *European Elements in Afro-Asia.* The Mankind Quarterly. January, (1964)

238. Bernard, Raymond W. From Chrishna to Christ. (1966)

239. Bal Gangadhar Tilak. *The Arctic Home in the Vedas.* (1903)

Images

Figure 1 - Scanned image of *New York Times*, September 29, 1931. Headline reads: "Piltdown Man Marks Dawn of Human Race, Osborn says, Contradicts Present Views"

Figure 2 - SPRINGFIELD REPUBLICAN, Massachusetts, November 22, 1953. "Piltdown Man Named Hoax, Jolts Science"

Figure 3 - Field Museum, Chicago, IL. Artistic display of "Lucy" (Australopithecus). Photo credit: Jovanna Goette

Figure 4 - Image showing complications that may appear during pregnancy concerning blood type.

Figure 5 - Scanned image of a Blood Parrot cichlid

Figure 6 - Yakow (Dzo) carrying goods near Lukla in Nepal. Photo credit: Nuno Nogueira

Figure 7 - This Cama has been created artificially by scientists using artificial insemination.

Figure 8 - In 2004, two grizzly-polar bear hybrid cubs were born at Osnabrück Zoo in Germany. Flickr: Christinas_Fotos

Figure 9 - Captive-bred gray wolf-coyote hybrid, Wildlife Science Center in Forest Lake, Minnesota.

Figure 10 - Diablo the Savannah Cat at Big Cat Rescue

Figure 11 - Wholphin, Sea Life Park Hawaii, Kekaimalu, born from a mating of bottlenose dolphin (mother), and a false killer whale.

Figure 12 - Side view of the Africanized honey bee

Figure 13 - Hercules, 922-Pound Liger, Is The World's Largest Living Cat, the hybrid offspring of a male lion and a tigress, at the Myrtle Beach Safari wildlife preserve in South Carolina.

Figure 14 - Fifteen species of howler monkeys are currently recognized. Previously classified in the family Cebidae, they are now placed in the family Atelidae.

Figure 15 - Found in Czechoslovakia, in 1891, and published in the National Geographic in October 1988. Eight centimeter high male head carved of mammoth ivory dated at 26,000 years BP.

Figure 16 - 30,000 year old Cro-magnon cave art from the Pyrenees

Figure 17 - Left: Star map showing Orion, Taurus, and Pleiades. Right: Cro-magnon cave art depicting a zodiac of stars and constellations.

Figure 18 - Cro magnon cave art from 15,000-30,000 BC

Figure 19 - "Falling Horse" painting by Cro magnon

Figure 20 - Paleolithic bone needles used for sewing during the ice age in Europe.

Figure 21 - 30,000 year old adult male burial in Sungir, Russia. Note the vast array of mammoth ivory beads that would have been attached to the clothing.

Figure 22 - Small ivory figurine of a female bird. Made from the tusk of a mammoth, it was found in 1908 at the Palaeolithic settlement of Mezin near the Russian border. On the torso of the bird is engraved an intricate pattern of joined up swastikas. It's the oldest identified swastika pattern in the world and has been radio carbon-dated to 15,000 years ago. National Museum of the History of Ukraine.

Figure 23 - Pleistocene map showing coast lines with sea levels 400 feet lower, as they were during parts of the ice age.

Figure 24 - Top image: Horse head from Mas d'Azil, about 15 000 BP. Bottom image: Engraved right metatarsal bone of reindeer depicting horse heads, from Le Mas d'Azil. Middle/Upper Magdalenian, ca 15 000 . Edouard Piette excavations, 1887-1894.

Figure 25 - Scanned image of a map of Atlantis. From *Atlantis, the Antediluvian World*, by Ignatius Donnelly, [1882]

Figure 26 - Scanned image From Le Mas d'Azil. Below the deer is a row of 13 dots, ending in a square.

Figure 27 - Scanned image From Le Mas d'Azil. Below the horse is a row of 29 dots, a lunar cycle.

Figure 28 - Map showing Europe and British Isles.

Figure 29 - Pharaoh before Horus,the Falcon-God. Temple of Sobek and Horus, Kom Ombo. This was one of the "healing" temples, to which pilgrims came to regain their health.

Figure 30 - Scanned image of a map showing the mid-Atlantic ridge, when sea levels were much lower during the ice age.

Figure 31 - Map showing the distribution of Clovis spear point technology. Notice the density is heaviest on the east, compared to the north west, where they supposedly originated from.

Figure 32 - British Museum. "Ginger", 5,500 year old naturally mummified remains, oldest found in Egypt to date.

Figure 33 - Map showing the geographic distribution of Haplotype X, on both sides of the Atlantic ocean.

Figure 34 - Scanned image of Rh negative mother pregnant with an Rh positive fetus.

Figure 35 - Map showing the geographic density of Rh negative people in Europe.

Figure 36 - All Canary Island pyramids are constructed from lava-stones and dated in 19 century AD. Thor Heyerdahl suggested that the structures were not haphazardly piled-up stones and maintained a belief in the hypothesis that the pyramids were connected with Guanches until his death. According to the Heyerdahl theory, even not so ancient Guanches (in 19th century) had an ancient culture of pyramid construction in the type of Mesoamerican pyramids and their knowledge for making pyramids similar in form.

Figure 37 - Scanned image of Madame H. P. Blavatsky

Figure 38 - Swastika symbols from cultures around the world.

Figure 39 - pre-Columbian Hopewell Green-slate Serpent Swastika

Figure 40 - Scanned image of Swastika constructed from Hebrew letters.

Figure 41 - Scanned image of a swastika-adorned vessel that dates to the early Moche-Sican-Lambayeque period, beginning around 100 B.C., and currently on display in the Huaca Rajada Site Museum in Peru.

Figure 42 - Scanned image of a Guanche mummy. Museum of Anthropology, Madrid, Spain.

Figure 43 - Guanche Mummy, Tenarife, Canary Islands.

Figure 44 - Public textbook from Mexico.

Figure 45 - Scanned image from Cuzco, Peru.

Figure 46 - El Castillo, Spanish for "the castle", also known as the Temple of Kukulcan, is a Mesoamerican step-pyramid that dominates the center of the Chichen Itza archaeological site in the Mexican state of Yucatan.

Figure 47 - Image showing the Linguistic similarities of Aryan languages.

Figure 48 - T Shaped Limestone Pillars at Göbekli Tepe 11th Millennium BC. Sanliurfa, Turkey

Figure 49 - Scan of image map showing the linguistic expansion of Aryans

Figure 50 - Sumerian, Early Dynastic period (ca. 2900–2350 B.C.), British Museum

Figure 51 - Scan of satellite images of pyramids in China. Google maps.

Figure 52 - "The Beauty of Xiaohe," female mummy, ca. 1800 BCE. Photo provided

Figure 53 - Male "Cherchen Man" and Female Tarim Mummies, ca. 1800 BCE.

Figure 54 - Female Tarim mummy with blonde braided hair, 1800 BCE.

Figure 55 - Scanned drawing of Genghis Khan

Figure 56 - Photo source: National geographic (June 2014)

Figure 57 - A scanned image of Egyptian Omphalos

Figure 58 - Scanned image of Mayan Long Count calendar

Figure 59 - photo credit: Atlantean Gardens

Figure 60 - The central medallion depicts a bull-slaying scene. Around the border are 12 signs of the zodiac. The sun ('Sol') and moon ('Luna') are depicted in the top corners, the two wind gods in the bottom. The inscription indicates that "Ulpius Silvanus, initiated into a Mithraic grade at Orange, France, paid his vows to Mithras". From Walbrook Mithraeum in Londinium, AD 180-220, Museum of London

Figure 61 - Graph of the Aryan language tree

Figure 62 - King Tut on Chariot. Painting from Tutankhamun's painted chest. Cairo Museum, Egypt.

Figure 63 - Photo Credit: Robert Sepehr

Figure 64 - Lion man of the Hohlenstein Stadel. A lion-headed figurine found in Germany and dating to the Upper Paleolithic. (about 40,000 BCE)

Figure 65 - Right: Scanned image of a Hexagram as part of a Mandala from Tibet. 19th century, Vajrayogini at the center, Rubin Museum of Art. Left: Scanned image of Slavic Swastika

Figure 66 - Robert Sepehr, Pergamon Museum, Berlin, Germany

Figure 67 - Tympanum of St. Trophime portal

CPSIA information can be obtained
at www.ICGtesting.com
Printed in the USA
LVHW080805060922
727646LV00024B/466